MOTHER ANGELICA'S ANSWERS, NOT PROMISES

MOTHER M. ANGELICA
WITH CHRISTINE ALLISON

POCKET BOOKS

New York   London   Toronto   Sydney   Tokyo   Singapore

All quotations from Holy Scripture are taken from *The Jerusalem Bible*, 1966 edition.

POCKET BOOKS, a division of Simon & Schuster Inc.
1230 Avenue of the Americas, New York, NY 10020

ISBN: 0-671-74673-1

First Pocket Books printing March 1988

10 9 8 7 6 5

POCKET and colophon are registered trademarks of
Simon & Schuster Inc.

Printed in the U.S.A.

In a Skeptical Age, Mother Angelica Is an Inspiration!

Mother Angelica reaches out to troubled people everywhere. On her own program, "Mother Angelica Live," her practical answers to life's real problems have won her a devoted audience of faithful fans. More than 15 million of Mother's spiritual booklets have been distributed throughout the world. And on "60 Minutes," the "Today" show, "Good Morning America" and other nationally syndicated programs, her vitality, humor and wisdom have inspired millions more. Now, *MOTHER ANGELICA'S ANSWERS, NOT PROMISES* offers the treasures of her joyous faith and hard-won experience to all of us who seek the answers to life's dilemmas, large and small.

"MORE AND MORE PEOPLE HAVE LEARNED— OFTEN THE HARD WAY—THAT THE PROMISES OF THIS WORLD ARE EMPTY PROMISES. ALL THE MONEY IN THE WORLD CAN'T HELP WHEN A LOVED ONE DIES. ALL THE FAME IN THE WORLD COUNTS FOR NOTHING WHEN A CHILD BECOMES ADDICTED TO DRUGS. AND YOU CAN HAVE FRIENDS AS NUMEROUS AS THE STARS AND BE AS ALONE AS THE MOST DESPERATE CREATURE WHO EVER LIVED. I DON'T BELIEVE IN THE PROMISES OF THIS WORLD. I BELIEVE IN *ANSWERS*. THAT'S WHY I WROTE THIS BOOK."

—Mother Angelica

MOTHER ANGELICA'S ANSWERS, NOT PROMISES

A Literary Guild Alternate Selection
A Doubleday Book Club Alternate Selection
A Catholic Digest Book Club
Alternate Selection

This book is lovingly dedicated to
Ginny Dominick Kelly, without whom it would
not have been conceived or completed.

Acknowledgments

No words could ever express my gratitude to all those who helped me in the writing of this book. Christine Allison, my coauthor, listened to many hours of tapes, viewed live shows, and pored over notes and other books I have written for all the material we used in it. Her tireless dedication and perseverance carried this book through its many phases and brought it to a successful conclusion. Ginny Dominick Kelly worked on composition and rewriting. Her encouragement renewed my hope when my spirit lagged. I am also grateful to John Boswell for his enthusiasm and counsel. My nuns' prayers kept us going and their generosity allowed me to spend so much time writing it.

Special thanks to Bill Steltemeier for his advice and encouragement, Sister M. Raphael for indexing, researching, and typing scores of papers, and Sister M. Antoinette for days and nights of typing and editing manuscripts and for her invaluable suggestions. Additionally, Sister M. Gabriel, O.P., and Father Don McDonagh were most helpful in critiquing and proofreading for theological content. Finally, Brad Miner convinced me of the need for this book and assured me there were people by the thousands who would begin new lives reading its pages.

I am most grateful to all these people for their unique contributions to this project. Most of all I thank the Lord God for giving me answers to so many questions.

Contents

THE BEGINNING

PART I. FIRST THINGS

PART II. LIFE AND LOVE

CONTENTS

PART III. LAST THINGS

THE
BEGINNING

Y OU MAY BE a bit surprised to be reading a book by a nun. Actually, that makes two of us. Because a nun is the one thing I never wanted to be.

As a child, I remember sitting in church in Canton, Ohio, watching the Sisters pray. The headpieces of their habits were so enormous that they blocked my view of the priest celebrating Mass. And their facial expressions were so sour that I was convinced they were the most unhappy people I'd ever seen. I even remember praying, "Lord, I'll never be one of those."

But the Lord works in mysterious ways. Because now I am a nun, and I've been one for forty-three years.

I am a cloistered nun. That means that instead of teaching or nursing or engaging in other professions, my life is devoted to prayer. Prayer takes many forms, and the center of my prayer is Adoration of the Holy Eucharist. The strength that I receive from Jesus in the Eucharist enables me to carry out the mission God has entrusted to me. That mission includes being faithful to my monastic life. It also includes

13

being involved in a work that's a little unusual for a nun, a work that takes me a few hundred steps from our little monastery to a television studio in our back yard—the Eternal Word Television Network (EWTN). After the usual preparations, I sit before the cameras to host a live program that is beamed by satellite to millions of homes across America.

That program led to this book. Each night when I'm on the air we open up the phone lines to receive calls from viewers. The calls come from every section of the country, from as many men as women, from people of every conceivable faith and every walk of life. After five years of fielding these calls I've gotten to know, in a general way, the people who make them. I call them my EWTN family. They do not call to make grand statements or to get into arguments or to show off. They call to ask questions.

I don't think they call to ask me questions because I'm a nun. In fact, as many Protestants call as Catholics. It may be because I'm a woman, and people find it easier to ask questions of a woman.

The questions are rarely easy. A little boy may want to know why his father died. A wife may want to know how to forgive a husband who abused their child. A lot of questions have to do with the burden of loneliness.

People who call with those kinds of questions, I learned quickly, won't settle for replies that are trite or out of a manual. Our catechism answers a lot of questions but it doesn't answer these. And the television equivalent of a pat on the back and promise that everything will turn out for the best won't cut it with my television family.

They've heard too many promises. Like more and more Americans, these callers have learned—often the hard way—that the promises of this world are empty promises. All the money in the world can't help when a loved one dies. All the fame in the world counts for nothing when a child becomes addicted to drugs. You can have friends as numerous as the stars and be as alone as the most desperate creature who ever lived.

I don't believe in the promises of this world.

I believe in <u>answers</u>.

I believe there <u>are</u> answers.

All I do every night I'm on the air is tell my family where to find them.

That's why I wrote this book, to share what my television family and I have discovered together.

WHY I DO WHAT I DO

To people in the media, a nun with her own television network makes a good story. So journalists from all over the world make the trip to Birmingham to confirm with their own eyes that, yes, we are real nuns, and yes, we have a real television studio, a real satellite dish, and all the components of real-world broadcasting.

If that's what they're looking for, they find it. But I want them to find something more.

In many circles television evangelists have gotten a bad name. Maybe in some cases it's deserved. But in most cases the critics don't understand the terrible hunger these evangelists are trying to feed. In any case the controversy has produced one notable side effect: it has made journalists skeptical of anyone who mixes television and religion.

Last year we had the pleasure of a visit from Morley Safer and a crew from CBS's *60 Minutes*. Perhaps you saw the segment they did when it aired. After many minutes of casual conversation, including a tour of our facilities, Morley Safer and I sat down for an interview. His first few questions were softballs. But then he decided to get down to hard cases. He wanted to know about money.

I am a Franciscan, which means I follow Jesus according to the example of the great Saint Francis of Assisi. He founded our Order, and when he did he required that all of his followers take a vow of poverty. Morley and I had just taken a walk through room after room jammed with the latest electronic equipment, millions of dollars' worth of up-to-date technology. "How," he asked, "can you square that with your vow of poverty?"

I think that's a fair question to ask of anyone who uses the means of this world to talk to people about the next world. The answer is that I do not own any of the equipment at the network, nor do I receive a salary. Our benefactors have been most generous in donating the money that has paid for EWTN. But all of the network, every nut, bolt, and videotape, belongs to God. Of course, we have a staff of paid professionals who operate the network, but EWTN is a nonprofit organization. The vow of poverty that the nuns and I make enables us to utilize the technology God makes available to us, knowing all the while that everything is His.

Happily, just as Morley Safer was asking his question, we were broke. I say "happily" because being broke is the secret of our success. Being broke, we need help. Needing help, we turn to God. Being constantly broke, we are constantly turning to God. Our message, the message we send out nightly across America, is about a loving God on Whom we can totally rely.

For if God decided to stop using us, we'd be off the air in two seconds.

When I told all this to Morley, at first he gave me a lifted eyebrow in response. But soon after, his look of skepticism dissolved into a smile. He was seeing firsthand God's Providence at work.

HOW I CAME TO BE HERE

A lot of people wonder how I ended up founding a monastery in the South and starting a Catholic cable network. As hard as it is for people to imagine, I never planned to do either of these things. I have always been very grateful for my vocation as a nun, and I've never desired any life but the one God gave me. In fact, I consider it one of God's greatest miracles in my life that He has allowed EWTN to prosper while preserving the fullness of my life as a nun. It may be hard to understand, but I've never had great dreams of ministry that I set out to pursue. I never started anything knowing what the whole game plan would be, or even how a project would be accomplished.

Instead, I've delighted in watching God evolve great things out of nothing. I believe firmly in allowing God to open doors and in stepping out in faith when He does so. Often those steps don't make any sense—not to me, and certainly not to a logical or reasonable observer. But I wouldn't want to live my life any other way. It excites me to watch what God is going to do next, and to see how He uses the small, seemingly insignificant occurrences in life to build the foundation for great things.

An example of His Providence is how I came to Birmingham. It began on a peaceful morning in our Order's monastery in Canton, Ohio. My assignment for the day was to clean and polish floors. For this job we used a power machine with hand controls and a rotary brush. By a freak accident the machine hit a slick spot, and before I could release the control bar, it spun out of control. It threw me against the wall, and I hit exactly at the one place in my spine that had been weakened by a birth defect.

The accident left me in great pain. After two years, my back had deteriorated to the point where surgery was required. According to the doctor, the odds were only fifty-fifty that I'd ever walk again.

I'll tell you exactly what my reaction was when he told me. I was petrified.

I remember lying in my hospital bed after the doctor explained the details of the intense operation and the risks associated with it. I stared at the gray-white wall. "Lord," I said, "if you'll let me walk again, I'll build you a monastery in the South."

Why the South? Your guess is as good as mine. All I know is that the operation was a success, and after therapy I began to walk again with the help of a back brace and a leg brace, which are my companions to this day.

The problem with making a bargain with God is that you have to hold up your end of it. I explained this to my mother superior and that great woman told me to go ahead. I gathered together five nuns and began making plans to build a monas-

tery in the South—in Birmingham, Alabama, to be precise—
the same Birmingham, Alabama, that at the time boasted a
Catholic population of exactly 2 percent.

I don't think anyone could have prepared those lovely Al-
abamians for our habits, homemade sandals, and the grille
that we erected to separate our cloister from visitors. I look
back on those days with wonderment; we weren't afraid to
ask for anything and we weren't afraid to get "no" for an
answer. But somehow we were always getting "yeses" from
the people of Birmingham, especially from the Italian community.

One man donated all the cement block for the monastery.
Another did the excavating and blasting of all the rock sur-
rounding the property. A woman and her daughter donated
all the brick. Near the end, when the building frame was up
but only half finished and we had run out of money, the
workmen lent us their time until we could repay them. And
from the start, one very special man, Joe Bruno, has provided
us with all our food and groceries.

As more people heard about us and our new building, more
began to drop by, some out of curiosity, others to see if they
could help. Before long we were receiving extraordinary support from both the Catholic community and the other Christian and Jewish congregations of Birmingham.

Having made a bargain with God, the nuns and I relied on
Him to enable us to fulfill our end of it. Through unexpected
people at unexpected moments, He showed us that when we
leaned on Him we could not fall.

When the building was up and the roof was on, we did
everything we could think of to raise money to sustain the
monastery. We even tried roasting peanuts to sell at local
sporting events and fairs. We were roasting peanuts by the
bushel and beginning to meet our expenses when the local
distributor came over to visit one day. He said we were going
to have to "grease a few palms" if we wanted to make it in
the roasting business. Imagine somebody saying that to a nun!
I told him that if I were going to hell, it surely wouldn't be
over peanuts.

It was several years later that the Lord showed us that He

had something else in mind for the monastery. By the early 1970s, our community had grown to twelve nuns. We bought some printing presses and began a book ministry. Our goal was to send the message of God's Goodness everywhere we could, and soon we were distributing over 500,000 books and booklets a month all over the world.

The little books were popular right from the beginning, and they led to requests for broadcast interviews, mostly on small, independent television stations. One such request came from Channel 38 in Chicago, and I obliged. And that's how I got into television.

Channel 38 was a small Christian station perched atop a tall building. There are hundreds of stations in the United States just like it. But for some reason, the moment I set foot inside that studio I said to myself, "Lord, I've got to have one of these!" This taught me something I've never forgotten. You've got to be very specific when you ask the Lord for something—you never know when He's going to pass by and say "Amen!"

But getting back to my story . . . for a few minutes I debated the obvious question: What on earth would twelve cloistered nuns do with a television station? It was a ridiculous idea. But so were our printing presses and the half-million books a month. By now I had learned to accept inspirations, even the crazy-sounding ones.

On the ride home from Chicago, I couldn't get the thought out of my mind. "Lord," I murmured to myself, "I've just got to have one of those."

A friend was driving the car. "What, Mother?" he asked. "One of what?"

"A television station or a studio or something," I said vaguely.

Just then, my companion Sister Joseph, who was sitting in the back seat praying, spoke up. "Mother, the Lord just said to me, 'Tell Mother the media is Mine and I give it to her.' "

"Are you joking?" I asked incredulously.

"I don't think He was," she answered.

That was the beginning of the Eternal Word Television Network. Through a series of modern-day miracles we received a charter from the FCC, support from wonderful and sometimes anonymous donors, backing from the local community—and, most importantly, guidance and courage from Our Lord. We went on the air in August 1981.

Those of you who receive our programming through your cable system know that ours has not been a fairy-tale ending, but it isn't supposed to be. And that's how God wants it. The struggles He has given us help us to trust Him more, to rely on Him more, and to remember what it is we're doing and why.

From monastery to publishing operation to the first Catholic satellite television network: it's a string that leads directly to the book you're holding. And it's my hope that, in reading this book, you will understand why I believe so strongly in the many things I want to tell you.

WHAT THIS BOOK IS ALL ABOUT

Our television audience keeps growing dramatically. Every time we add viewers to our EWTN family, we receive even more requests for tapes of particular shows. Our viewers write to us with their problems and tell us how much our tapes and shows help them in their daily lives. The questions and comments that come to us through the mail and on the *Live* show made us realize the need to provide answers, not promises.

Finally this year the nuns convinced me that we should put some of these answers down on paper. We tried to be as systematic as possible in coming up with the most frequently asked questions, and as we did so, we saw a sort of "trinity" emerge. There were questions that had to do with searching for God, getting to know Him, and finding out what He wills for us, which we grouped into a section called "First Things." Then there were those questions that had to do with the trials and rigors of faith in the real world, and those we grouped into a second section called "Life and Love." Finally, there were questions that centered on the next world, the world that people are sometimes afraid even to ask about. We called that section "Last Things."

In all probability you are wrestling with at least one of these questions right now, and if you are, I suggest you turn to that question first, read through the chapter, and then go back and start at the beginning to read the rest of the book at your leisure. I hope that it <u>isn't</u> a "real page-turner"—I'd rather that you take your time.

This book is a primer. The truths of Christianity have been around for two thousand years, and yet how little do we apply them to the world we live in, to the pains we suffer, and to the joys we let pass by. They are not easy truths. Christianity is not a "feel good" religion, nor is it a prescription for instant happiness. This is a book for all Christians, because it is based on the truths all Christians share.

WHAT GOD WANTS YOU TO BE

I wrote this book because I feel very strongly that God wants you to be a saint.

Don't be surprised.

And don't dismiss it.

Any one of us can be overwhelmed by the Presence of God in a beautiful cathedral while a choir is chanting. Any one of us can feel the special warmth of God that flows from an eloquent sermon or an evening prayer service.

But it takes holiness—a special grace—to resist choking your spouse when he or she humiliates you in public or lies to you or cheats on you.

A woman once said to me, "The problem with life is that it is so . . . <u>daily</u>."

Day in and day out, even as we are beset with the problems and questions of life, we are called to ask for that special grace of holiness. We are called to reject the empty promises of the world. We are called to embrace the answers that even now lie within our grasp.

If you can for a moment put aside the things that trouble

you, put aside the specific questions of your own life, then I'd like to ask you the deepest question of all. That question is, "Why do we search?"

The answer is: Because we are called to holiness, you and I, and we are not there. Not yet.

Come seek with me.
It isn't an easy road. It wasn't meant to be.
But it is our road, and we are called to travel it.

Part I

FIRST THINGS

— 1 —

Why Is It So Hard to Believe?

A FEW YEARS AGO, at the end of a grueling week right in the middle of our efforts to found the Eternal Word Television Network (EWTN), I gave a speech at a conference in Los Angeles. It was a long speech, and when I finished I felt tired and a little nauseated, so I went backstage and took a couple of Maalox. Suddenly, a woman came up from behind me and cried out, "Mother! You're supposed to have such great faith. Why do you need to take Maalox?" My stomach was really starting to feel upset. "Lady," I said, "I do have faith. It's just that my stomach doesn't know it."

Now what, you may wonder, does Maalox have to do with believing in God? Well, believing in God takes faith, and faith, for me, is like having one foot in the air, one foot on the ground, and a very queasy feeling in my stomach. Faith requires that you live your life in darkness, that you follow Someone Whom you cannot see and love Someone Whom you cannot touch. Some people find it ludicrous, others find it miraculous. But for me it's always been a matter of trusting His Word.

Faith is a fascinating subject, and I think that everyone has to confront or at least ponder the question of belief in God. A reasonable person simply cannot live an entire lifetime without asking himself why billions of people throughout history have worshiped a God Who is invisible, His Son, Who by mere appearances was a carpenter, and the Spirit, Whose Presence seems incomprehensible.

Every day, the network receives calls and letters from people searching for clear explanations of faith. Last summer I received a phone call from a woman who "didn't have time for idle conversation" and simply wanted me to send her four or five "convincing" proofs of God's existence by return mail so she could convert her son. I had to break the news to her that it wasn't going to be quite that simple. Asking why it is so hard to believe is like asking why you fall in love. There are no recipes, no shortcuts. God inspires you with a desire for Him, and slowly you begin to know that there is another Presence besides your own.

If you, too, are asking this question, then I know one very important thing about you: if pressed, you'd rather believe in God than not. Actually, I think that everyone, if given a choice, would prefer to know that there is a God, a God Who loves them and Whom he or she can love in return. The need to know and to love God is, at some level, as primary as the need to be fed and clothed. Those who do believe are sustained in immeasurable ways. Indeed, throughout history we see that where the spiritual needs of people were met, their material needs became easier to endure, simply because the Spirit upholds human beings in the face of adversity. If you are asking questions about faith, if you are seeking knowledge of God, then you have already begun to possess the very thing you feel you lack.

LOOKING FOR GOD IN ALL THE WRONG PLACES

We cannot live a full life without faith. Yes, we can get up in the morning and gulp down a bowl of cereal, drive to work in a daze, push a pencil for eight hours and come home at night—and call that living. But without faith, we cannot really be alive. People who have no faith live in a void. They have a strange sense of emptiness in their lives, a vacuum, a thirst that can send them around the world—to the heights of life and to its depths—in search of anything that can fill that void. But nothing will.

It is hard to find the fulfillment that comes only from God in a culture that places so much emphasis on "self." And yet this is the environment most people find themselves in. Modern philosophers unabashedly advocate "self-fulfillment" as not only the road to happiness but, in an odd way, an inalienable right. I find this especially sad because it leads so many away from faith in God.

I met a "master" of self-fulfillment a couple of years ago. Richard, a thirty-six-year-old lawyer from Illinois, to his surprise (and mine) found himself on our doorstep one day. Here was a man who had "everything" and plenty of it: power, prestige, position, as well as a wife he described as a "terrific lady" and two "super" kids. But all was not well with the man who had everything, for he also had a spiritual chip on his shoulder. His visit to the network was born out of a free-floating contempt for God as well as for anyone who loved God. In truth, Richard was desperately searching for God, although he disguised it in some pretty strange ways.

Richard wasted no time before insulting me. After a nasty remark about our Franciscan habit, he started interrogating me about monastic life and my "insane decision to escape the real world." If you've ever wanted to flatten a man twice your size, you know what it means to be Italian. Fortunately, the Lord interceded and suggested that I turn the tables and start asking Richard some questions. I obliged.

"You have a fine job and a beautiful family, don't you?"

I asked, as patiently as I could. "Of course I do," he responded shortly.

"Do you have any favorite pastimes?" I inquired. "Yes. I enjoy sailing and I like to jog every morning. So what?" he said.

"Do you ever travel?" I pressed. "Sure, I take my wife to Europe every year," he retorted.

"Do you have all the money that you think you will ever need?" I asked. "More than I'd ever admit to you!" he snapped.

"So you must be very happy," I said quietly.

It was then that Richard looked out the window with eyes that began to well up. "No, I'm not," he said haltingly, "and I can't stand the fact that you and all your nuns truly are happy."

Richard was discovering the hard truth: that he had been searching for the very thing he had been running from. The last thing he had ever wanted was for God to be the answer. He wanted to be self-sufficient, self-fulfilled, his own man, a man who owed nothing and answered to no one. Like so many of us, he had sought meaning in his work, his possessions, his "perfect" lifestyle. He poured everything he had into the "real world"—but the "real world" never gave back anything of lasting value.

We all know that on some level our escapes are not escapes at all. We immerse ourselves in workaholism or alcoholism or drugs or sin and end up dissatisfied and guilty. We bury our need for God in a thousand-and-one activities, chasing this promise and that promise—better skin, sharper minds, perfect dinner parties, exciting sports, and loving friends. But as "new and improved" as we can make ourselves, as much as Madison Avenue and Main Street U.S.A. have to offer, we still come up with an odd sort of restlessness. An uneasiness. A sadness that caused one woman to ask me in a letter, "Is there life after a new Rolls-Royce?"

There are countless roadblocks and detours to believing in God, and I guess that's one reason why it's so hard for some to believe in Him. It seems like the more you want to know Him, the harder you look in all the wrong places. Show me a woman who goes from relationship to relationship, or an executive who lives in the fast lane, or a teenager who is addicted to music videos, or a scientist who spends every waking moment in his lab, and I'll show you someone who is desperately trying to dodge God. Some of these people successfully block God from their whole lives. But for others who stop long enough to reflect, they begin to feel a thirst that is unquenchable. This restlessness becomes so over-whelming that they are forced to reckon with the awesome possibility that there might be something or Someone Who is greater than anything or anyone else they have known, that there might be a way to make sense out of it all, after all.

"IS THIS ALL THERE IS?"

If you think that everyone who believes in God has been struck down by lightning, guess again. Faith, for most of us, comes in tiny, ordinary steps, and the first step is generally an impatience with the world as we know it. "Wait just a minute, everybody. This can't be all there is," we say to any and all who will listen. Life, as we know it, has become an absurdity—or is about to. When we experience that faint thirst that makes us aware, "There's a vacuum inside me; some-thing's missing," we are being called.

Most of us would attribute this discontent to the sophisti-cation of our own minds, or to the influence of a theologian or philosopher or friend. We might think that the emptiness we feel is an emptiness of our own making, and at this point we have no reason to know that it is something far more exciting, far more important. Because, in truth, the emptiness is not just part of being human, but is permitted by God for a special purpose. It is God calling us to Him, letting us know that as hard and fast as we look, we will never again be satisfied until we know and believe in Him. It is God working through the people around us and in everything we see and hear and read. As Saint Paul writes in his letter to the Gala-tians, "Then God, Who had specially chosen me while I was still in my mother's womb, called me through His Grace and chose to reveal His Son in me'' (Galatians 1:15). The call that God directed to Saint Paul is also directed to you and me. It is His gift to us. When we understand that God has called us individually by name, it profoundly alters the way we live.

What most of us don't realize is that you and I were made by God to know, love, and serve Him. We weren't created just to eat, drink, and be merry. Nor were we created only to punch a time clock or whatever else it is that we do every day. No, our primary mission in life, the answer to ''Why are we alive?'' is to love and serve God. This is not to say that everything else we do in life isn't good and holy. We weren't all meant to wear Franciscan habits or to serve in soup kitchens or to do missionary work in South America. Whatever our present state in life may be, the key is that we accept and understand that our real purpose in life is to be God-centered rather than self-centered.

Once we recognize this truth, we begin to see that emptiness, restlessness, and thirst are inevitable whenever we distance ourselves from God. We can now understand that mid-life crises are born of the fact that we've spent half a lifetime barking up the wrong tree! Our understanding of youth is broadened when we see teenage rebellion as the raw, unbridled search for the extraordinary amidst the ordinary. Boredom with this life is merely an exhaustion with the fruits of this world and the need to grapple with the reality of the Infinite. We were made for God, and without Him we are going to be out of kilter, dissatisfied, and quietly desperate. The person who accepts the fact that he belongs to God has taken the most important step to believing.

WHO IS GOD, ANYWAY?

I guess that any discussion about believing in God should begin with general agreement on Whom we are talking about. This is where many of us trip and fall and never get up again.

Many expect God to be a grandfather in fine white robes Who either corrects harshly or just overlooks our existence.

You see, our problem is one of perception. You and I operate with finite minds in a material world. This is fine for grocery shopping and putting bandages on children's knees and playing bridge on Saturday night. But the finite mind is somewhat of a drawback in perceiving an Infinite Being in the world of the supernatural. God doesn't breathe down our necks, either; He is devoted to allowing us to exercise our own free wills, but a lot of us take that as proof positive that He doesn't exist! How easy it is to avoid the Truth. Because as long as you seek that "great granddaddy in the sky" rather than the God Who loves you as though no one else existed, you're going to be disappointed. What a tragic mistake!

At first, we all seek a "God of the senses," a God we can see and hear and touch. We formulate this image as children, and it is an important first step in knowing the fatherliness of our God. But unfortunately, for many, the learning curve hits a plateau with that image, and we grow into adulthood looking for that same "old man." Then when He doesn't come to rescue us from our financial crises or when He doesn't save a loved one from death, we write Him off as one of the many last resorts that never came through.

The truth is that God is invisible. You can't see Him. You can't hear Him. You can't touch Him. But He is there. He always was and He always will be. He knows everything and everyone because He created everything and everyone. There isn't a thing that goes on without God knowing it. God's greatness is incomprehensible to us, but our inability to grasp it does nothing to change the fact that it is true. The challenge of belief is to step outside the confines of our own senses and to grasp, on some level, this Truth that we cannot see or hear or hold.

WHY WON'T HE SPEAK UP?

If our *Mother Angelica Live* show is any indication, one of the things that bugs people most about God is that He is always silent. You wouldn't believe how many people call in to complain about it. "How am I supposed to believe in Someone Who never speaks to me?" "How do I know if He's heard my prayer?" "Why won't God just come right out and tell me the answer to my problem?" they ask. Without trying to be funny, I tell them to <u>listen</u>. That's a tough notion, because we usually presume that silence means absence. We figure that since we have voices, then God must have a louder Voice! This is a good example of how our finite minds can get us into a lot of trouble.

About twelve years ago, I went to the hospital for tests, and for some reason they put me in a room all the way down at the end of an empty corridor. It was extremely quiet. Almost like another world. I was aware that this was not just an ordinary quiet—it was a different kind of silence. I wasn't used to it at all. For the first few days, I prayed constantly and read Scripture aloud. Then, gradually, the silence became my friend. I came to realize that, in spite of the silence, I was not alone. God's silent Presence was becoming intensely apparent to me.

What I experienced in that noiseless room was that God does not work in noise and commotion. He works in absolute quiet. I became increasingly aware that His ever-present act of Creation is a silent one, whether it is the forming of a child in a mother's womb or a blade of grass breaking through the earth. I realized as I lay there that atoms were shifting all around me, within me, over me and under me, all in utter silence. I thought of the tons of snow that fall each year without anyone hearing a sound. And how the planets spin and revolve without as much as a whisper.

God was showing me how He operates, plain and simple, in silence. Now, I realize that it takes time and faith to know that silence is, in fact, the sound of His Presence. But if you just take a few minutes every day to stop and <u>listen to the</u>

silence, you will begin to be more aware of God's Presence. As Scripture says, "Be still and know that I am God" (Psalms 46:10). If you make it your business to listen for Him, you will become keenly aware that He is there. All you really have to do is stay quiet long enough to hear Him speak within the silence of your heart.

Ever since my stay in the hospital, I have recommended silence as a pathway to believing in God, because in silence you really have to face yourself and Whoever is there with you. It is said that Saint Francis de Sales was once gazing at a rose and became so keenly aware of God's perfect Hand in the making of it that he cried out, "Stop shouting!" Once we attune ourselves to silence, we learn that it is not just the absence of noise. It is the Presence of God Himself.

SO HOW CAN I GET TO KNOW GOD?

Now that you know God has chosen you, and that He wants you to believe, you can see your restlessness and thirst as additional signs of His existence and Love for you. "But Mother, so far you've only got me hungering for the Silent One somewhere in the darkness. It's still hard to believe."

Yes, these are the toughest moments for the aspiring believer! But they are not as tough as you might think. Remember, your belief in God is something that God has already willed for you. It is a gift. Not that you deserve it, mind you. Neither do I. Nobody ever receives it because of merit. It is not a medal we receive for good conduct. It is a gift of love freely given to us that we may choose to accept or reject.

How do we go about accepting this precious gift? By a leap in faith. It is at this point that you've either got to ride the horse or get off it. The leap should not be taken in a moment of emotionalism, but with the quiet courage that separates the men from the boys and the sheep from the goats. This is not a time to panic, but rather a time to humbly ask God for the courage you need to accept the gift He has already given you. God is not going to leave you stranded in the darkness, nervously twiddling your thumbs. But He does expect you to <u>ask</u> Him for the light that only He can give.

He will give you this light through three very powerful tools, and though I'm sure you are familiar with the words that identify them, you might not know what they truly mean. The words are Faith, Hope, and Love. And what they mean is the complete transformation of your life.

The process of believing in God is just that, a process, a spiritual journey that has a tangible beginning and a mystical end. Every step of the journey is possible with these three virtues at your side. Faith, Hope, and Love are the virtues that take you from being a spiritual bystander to being a believer.

- Faith is what gets you started.
- Hope is what keeps you going.
- Love is what brings you to the end.

Now I know that when I say "Faith, Hope, and Love" you may be tempted to wrinkle your nose, fearing that we're about to discuss some hard-to-understand theological treatise. They sound like words, just words, and you can't imagine that they could ever make a difference in your life. But they are far more than just words—they are precious gifts given to you by God, infused in you at Baptism, so that you might come to know Him. "It looks like I'm about to become terribly confused," you think to yourself. But if you'll give me a chance, I'll show you how Faith, Hope, and Love will finally fill the void in your life. And finally you will be able to live in peace.

First, let's discuss faith. What does faith mean to us? On a natural level, it means a kind of confidence or trust. We have faith in our ability to perform certain duties. We ask our spouse to be faithful to us. We accept an IOU in good faith. Natural faith relies on the actions of ourselves and others, and so it is riddled with imperfections and disappointments.

But faith in God, which we call Supernatural Faith, and which is implanted into our souls at Baptism, is founded on God rather than on ourselves. Supernatural Faith helps us to know that what God has revealed to us is true. With this kind of faith comes an attitude of acceptance. This doesn't mean that we know everything about God or about what He has revealed. But it does mean that we know that God exists without looking for scientific evidence or material proofs— that He loves us, and that He has our best good at heart, no matter how bleak or confused our circumstances may be. It is through Supernatural Faith that we can see His work in darkness.

A good friend of the network once told us about a debate he had with an atheist. Not surprisingly, they were arguing about the existence of God.

The atheist said, "Prove to me that there's a God and I'll become a Christian."

"Oh, no, you don't," the priest replied. "You're in the minority in this world. You prove to me that there isn't a God and I'll become an atheist!"

"Well, I can't," the atheist said.

"What?" he replied. "You believe in something that you can't prove? My dear, that means you have faith. Faith is believing in something you can't prove. And if you're right, if there is no God, you're never going to know it. But if I'm right, and there is a God, you're going to know it forever and ever!"

Well, I had to chuckle when the priest told us that story, but he wasn't just being clever. Supernatural Faith, as he pointed out, is seeing in darkness what we will someday see in light. No doubt about it: we're going to do a lot of groping in this life. As we move forward on our spiritual journey, our faith will have its ups and downs. But that's okay. Even doubt can make us grow and increase our faith in God. If we keep acting in faith even when we doubt, our faith will have the opportunity to make great strides toward God. Some days we will be filled with enormous conviction. Other days, we won't be so sure. The point is just to keep trying.

But you say, "Mother, when I see someone suffering, I can only see that person and his pain. How can I know God is there?"

It is faith that tells you He is there. It takes time, of course.

Sometimes your human reason tells you something is ridiculous, or unfair, or just doesn't make any sense. Like the tragic death of a child, or losing your job, or your marriage breaking up. At times like these, it takes faith to know that God is with you, even in the midst of such a terrible circumstance. That He has some purpose for this tragedy, as painful as it might be. That He permits it in order to bring about some greater good, which you may not become aware of until many years later.

For example, let's imagine a man—we'll call him Joe—who is out of work and who's had an offer for a fifty-thousand-dollar-a-year job. He starts out an hour early for the final interview. As he is driving up a hill, there is a drunk driver, weaving back and forth on the far side of the hill, who will run a stop sign at the very moment Joe passes through the intersection. Except that suddenly, Joe's own car begins to weave—he has blown a tire. He manages to get off to the side of the road, but he is heartsick. He has no spare, and there are no other cars in view. He waits and waits, misses the interview, and loses the job. All because of a flat tire. He becomes bitter. If he hadn't lost the job, he would have been able to care for his elderly parents, pay off his debts, and have a much easier life. His logic sees no sense to the incident. But what Joe does not see is that his very life was spared from a head-on collision. His reason can only understand what his senses perceive; he has no way of knowing all the factors that were involved. He thinks this was a cruel blow on God's part.

This is where faith comes in. There is in God a Permitting Will and an Ordaining Will. His Permitting Will sometimes does allow adversity in our lives, but will always bring a greater good out of it. You can see the greater good in this story—God sparing Joe from a fatal accident. But Joe has to depend on faith.

If you realize that God is operating from the vantage point of eternity, and that His Plan for you concerns your life in the next world as well as this one, then you will be more attuned to Him. Then your humility will allow you to pray.

You will be able to tell Him, "I don't know You; I can't find You, but I want to."

And then, suddenly, in the midst of a painful or unpleasant situation, you will experience a tremendous increase in faith, and your desire for God will grow. The painful incident may not change, but you will have the courage to bear with it, without bitterness. In my own life, if we had looked at the "fact" of twelve nuns who barely knew how to adjust the color on a television set, we would never have built our first television studio. If we had looked at the "fact" that satellite dishes cost money (and we only had $200), we would never have started a network. There are no limits to what God can accomplish. That is reality. And when we ask for something that is in accordance with His Will, it is always granted. I'm not suggesting that you should expect from God a Cadillac when you can only afford roller skates. You must remember that God doesn't give us everything we want simply because of faith. Faith obtains for us only what is within the Plan of God, only what will be for our good.

Hope is the second extraordinary virtue we receive at Baptism. It is not the natural kind of hope we all talk about, as in "I hope I win the lottery" or "I hope little Danny passes his exam." These are examples of hope on a natural level, which always contains an element of doubt. We're not sure we're going to get what we hope for. But Supernatural Hope is not about some future unfulfilled expectations; it is based on the firm, solid knowledge we have of God's Goodness and Power in the present moment. Supernatural Hope is a spirit of courage and strength. It gives us the assurance that our God, Who is invisible, is real and keeps His promises.

Supernatural Hope assures us that we possess God now; we don't have to wait until we get to Heaven to possess the One we love, desire, and want to know. This assurance gives us the strength, power, and grace to endure whatever is happening in our lives, regardless of the circumstances.

Take the case of a woman we'll call Edna, who is dealing with her husband's terminal illness. On a natural level, she fervently hopes her husband will be restored to full health.

But, mindful of the diagnosis, she knows the chances of his recovery are not good. As she endures his long months of suffering, she may become resentful and bitter and finally come to despair. Natural hope gives her nothing to hang on to.

Without Supernatural Hope, Edna can only view the situation on a human level. At this time she is in great need of Supernatural Hope, which would give her an awareness of God's Presence in the midst of all the pain. She would know that she is not alone. She would have the ability to pray with confidence that God will restore her husband to health. But she would also have the freedom to accept the long hours of pain, and possibly his death, without becoming devastated. This may seem contradictory, but Supernatural Hope is the balance between expecting a miracle and accepting God's Will even if it results in pain and death. There is a certain serenity that comes from Supernatural Hope, a serenity that enables us to persevere with the assurance of God's Love.

Hope tells us to move along, that it's all right, God is at our side, and that no matter what the appearances, regardless of the fact that we can't see Him or hear Him, He is here, right now, with us and in us. When we pray for hope, it will be given to us in large measure, to sustain us through tragedies, injustices, and uncertainties. Hope gives us joy in sorrow and peace amidst the turmoil of daily life. In certain ways, I think it is the virtue we need most of all.

Finally, there is love. We all know what love is on a natural level; it is, more often than not, a love of the senses. A young man and woman meet, fall in love, and marry because she was peaceful and calm and he had a great sense of humor. A year later, she's a bore and he's a tiresome wisecracker. It is love on a natural level that can become very selfish, because it only wants to keep and receive. But Love on a Supernatural level, with God as its source, only asks to give and to share.

Supernatural Love is God's Love in our soul. The person who possesses Supernatural Love is able to keep loving when reason says it's time to give up. It's what makes us able to forgive, and to keep forgiving, when what we really want to do is throw in the towel and be forever angry at the person who keeps hurting us. When Jesus commanded that we love our enemies, He knew that to do so we'd have to possess Supernatural Love. He knew that loving our enemies requires looking beyond what we feel like doing, what we are "justified" in doing, and instead being very compassionate and understanding.

On an even more practical level, Supernatural Love is what enables you to keep loving your spouse or your children or your best friend when at the moment you are hard pressed to find anything lovable about them. It allows you to keep in mind that everyday annoyances that can drive you crazy—the unmade bed, the car left on empty, the squeezing of the toothpaste tube in the middle, the monopolizing of the TV's remote control—are small items in the overall scope of things. How? By making you aware that <u>love is a decision</u>, not just a feeling, and that you can decide to love as God loves—freely and endlessly.

Supernatural Love is the kind of love that keeps marriages vibrant, families solid, friendships strong. It's the kind of love that inspires Christians to true acts of kindness and charity. Supernatural Love doesn't judge or ask questions. It simply gives.

Love is the whole point of Christianity, because God is Love. The New Testament is a book of love, for love is what Jesus spoke of throughout His stay on earth. For the believer, the Commandment "Love one another as I have loved you" (John 15:12) is the measure of all things. It is Love that makes us truly Christian. If you're wondering how you measure up as a Christian, ask yourself: "Was I kind today?" "Was I compassionate today?" "Was I forgiving today?"

Faith, Hope, and Love all have a part to play in our process of knowing God. They are given to us in seed form for us to nurture and increase in our daily life. But for many of us they are just vague notions. They get buried, like marvelous treasures do, beneath mounds of earthly concerns. The important thing to remember about Faith, Hope, and Love is that they are transforming virtues. They mold us and chip away at our weaknesses until we are re-created in the Image of God. They aren't magic formulas, but mysteries. They don't make anyone a "true believer" or a "good person" overnight, but they give us the fortitude and the grace to slowly and deliberately experience God and to radiate that experience in our daily lives. The reason it is so hard to believe is that the invisible God must become the center of our lives. Believing in God takes a lifetime series of decisions in God's favor. It means not just knowing about God, but wanting to become just like Him.

TRUE BELIEVERS

If you and I decided to take a survey of our fellow Americans, the majority of them would say that they believe in God. What they really mean, though, is that they believe God exists. I'm sure God appreciates their vote of confidence. But this is where the believer and the spiritual bystander part ways. Simply believing in the existence of God is not exactly what I would call a commitment. After all, even the devil believes that God exists! Believing has to change the way we live.

A lot of people tell me they want to believe. But what they really want is a quick cure for all that ails them. They figure that Christianity makes one healthy, wealthy, and wise, and that once they profess belief in God, all their troubles will disappear. The problem is what happens when God says "No." What happens when life with all of its injustices and heartaches crowds in upon them and there seems to be no answer to their problems? This is where they need Faith to see God, Hope to hang on to Him, and Love to keep their souls in peace.

I will never forget one afternoon when a friend came into the network offices, asking if we could chat for a while. Rebecca is a talkative person, an accomplished attorney, always quick with the right answers and the best solutions. So I was puzzled when she sat down before me in complete silence.

She gazed around my office and her eyes settled on my book-case. It seemed like small talk wasn't in order, so I too was silent. Finally, she said, "Mother, you know I've been a churchgoer all my life, but I don't know what it means to really believe in God. I am absolutely panicked by the idea that if I really give in to Him, He's going to ask me to give up everything."

"Like what?" I asked gently, still a little confused about her problem.

"Like my new house, that's what!" she answered, choking on the horror of the thought.

Now I must explain that Rebecca has her own highly re-spected law practice and all the trappings of success: a new home, a late-model car, beautiful clothes. Still, I could not contain my laughter.

"God doesn't want your house—you don't even have cur-tains yet!" I exclaimed.

Well, she relaxed a bit, and we were able to figure out what was really bothering her. Rebecca, like so many others, had spent her entire life looking for the love and stability of God in a material existence. That intense search had caused her to achieve extraordinary success in her business life, and the love she wanted to give to God had been poured into all of her possessions instead. When she finally started to know God, she was caught between her old love for possessions and her new love for God. She just couldn't face the thought of losing everything.

But she had nothing to fear. God didn't want her posses-sions. He wanted her. It's true that some people are called to give up everything, but poverty is surely not a prerequisite for Christianity. There have been rich saints and poor saints and everything in between. Salvation is for everyone, not just for a chosen few.

Then why do so many resist accepting God's gift of faith? There are as many reasons for resisting belief and commit-ment to God as there are people whom He loves. But what mainly stands between us and true joy is our fear of the un-known.

- We don't know what will happen to us.
- We balk at the idea of putting someone else in charge.
- We cringe from what we imagine God will ask us to do.

I will never tell you that believing in God is easy, and if you are standing on the edge right now wondering whether or not to take the leap, I know exactly how you feel—because I, too, have had to make that decision, the decision to let go, over and over again. Faith will come to you, because God wants you to have it. If I, as an unhappy teenager in Canton, Ohio, could finally accept His gift, so can you. You don't have to become a nun or a Catholic, although the Church is a source of strength you won't find anywhere else. All you need to do is yield, with a humble heart, to God, Who loves you more than anyone does, can, or ever will. You will find that belief is not a onetime decision, but an ongoing, fascinating set of opportunities to say "Yes" to God, to jump again and again into those mystical Arms that your faith tells you are there. Granted, it requires taking a risk. But the more you say "Yes" to God, the easier it will become to take that risk.

GOD WANTS YOU

God wants to give you the gift of faith, even if you find the idea of a personal relationship with God frightening. You may even have been raised in a Christian faith, received Baptism, and still attend church regularly and yet feel far away from God. You'd like to experience Him in your life but don't really know how, and sometimes you're not even sure you really believe in Him. But God wants you. He is looking for you more than you are looking for Him. You may wonder, "Why is He hounding me?" All of us, at one point, wrestle with "why" He wants us, and "what" He'll ask us to do.

The poet Francis Thompson, who was a drug addict, is a good example of someone with these questions and fears. He a man with many problems. But even in the midst of his illness and weakness, God made Himself present. Along the way, Francis composed haunting poetry.

In "The Hound of Heaven," he wrote:

> I fled Him, down the nights and down the days;
> I fled Him, down the arches of the years;
> I fled Him, down the labyrinthine ways
> Of my own mind;
> And in the mist of tears
> I hid from Him . . .

Francis Thompson made one wrong choice after another. Yet God pursued him into the depths of his drug addiction. A soul never falls so low that God cannot raise it up, provided the soul is repentant. No matter what your circumstances, God is always seeking your love. When you say, "I want to know God," you are already beginning to feel His Hand on your shoulder. He is constantly after you even though you may think He has forgotten you.

At the end of the poem, the Voice of God says:

> All which I took from thee I did but take,
> Not for thy harms,
> But just that thou might seek it
> In My Arms.

I know this reality is difficult to grasp. It was difficult for me during my childhood to believe that God was pursuing me, that He loved me. When I was young my mother and father divorced, and life was miserable. In those days, many people in the Church and in my hometown disapproved of people who divorced, and as a child I bore the brunt of it.

When you are young, the one thing you don't want is to be an outsider. You want friends. You want acceptance. I was the only child in the entire school whose parents were divorced, so I always felt put in a corner as "someone different."

Sometimes I used to wonder if there was a God, and if

there was such a Person, I couldn't figure out why He wouldn't let me have a family like the other kids. I used to watch them go home at night to a great supper and lively conversation with their families, and wonder why my mother and I were worrying about where our next meal would come from. Yet I was too young to understand. I was only eight or nine years old. So it was impossible for me to understand how any of this could be part of a larger plan or even part of God's Love for me.

It took a while, but I later came to understand that God had been hounding me. He made Himself the first and last resort in my life. He even used my Italian temperament to bring me close to Him. At night I would pray: "God, I am angry inside. I hurt. Why must I go through all of this? I want to love You, but I don't know how."

With time, I could see how God was pulling me toward Him, helping me to know Him. My mother loved me, but she was a woman deeply hurt, rejected and crushed. We clung to each other without a friend to share our despair. But God was with us. Hidden. Quiet. Watching and waiting. Only later would I be ready to listen and give Him free reign in my soul.

LETTING GO

God will never stop hounding you until your last breath. You must never forget that God has chosen you, just as He chose me. Once you accept this gift of His Love, you will experience Him in your life. You will no longer want to be separated from Him. For He will have filled that vacuum in your heart with Himself.

It won't be filled any other way.

Yes, you can try to avoid God. You can run from Him by chasing after drugs or drink or sex or work or whatever else you've been cramming into your soul. But something will always seem wrong. Your soul, if it is filled with everything but God, will be like a car that is filled with water instead of gasoline. It simply won't work. You can say you're happy, but you'll always know that something is missing.

The Gospel of Saint Mark tells us about a man who was struggling with faith. He says to the Lord, "I do have faith. Help the little faith I have" (Mark 9:24). If you will just ask God to help you believe, your spiritual companions Faith, Hope, and Love will soon show you a very different world. As you become more attuned to the reality of God's existence and Love, you will begin to see the world as He sees it. And, with His Grace, you will begin to embrace holiness.

God has chosen you.
Believe in His Love.

—2—

What Does God Want with Me?

WHEN I WAS a young nun, I used to read the lives of the saints, hoping to find someone like me. Someone who had to eat six times a day and get nine hours of sleep. Someone who was not robust enough to make all the sacrifices that the "ordinary" saint seemed able to make. I read about saints who had spent entire nights in prayer and gone days without food. The more I looked, the more discouraged I became, realizing that holiness must be for the elite.

As I leafed through the pious and often boring biographies, I got the impression that saints were born saints; that they were creatures like angels, different from you and me from the very start. And the plaster-of-paris statues in our church just added to my confusion. The women were wide-eyed and graceful, while the men were gentle and handsome. There were no fat statues, no saints with big noses. None of the saints were frowning, and none looked tired.

Between the biographers and the artists, I was having a hard time imagining a saint's life, much less relating to it.

Before long, I was fed up. I wished then, and I wish now,

that the biographers of the saints would go to Purgatory for forty years. They made the saints unrealistic. They made them perfect. <u>Always</u> kind. <u>Always</u> patient. <u>Always</u> able to resist temptation.

What the biographers failed to note was that the majority of saints were ordinary people who struggled with temptations, sin, frailties, and weaknesses. Just like you and me.

Take the Apostles, for example. The men that Jesus chose to teach and to follow Him and to inspire others to follow Him were extremely imperfect. (Did you know that there is no account in Scripture of the Apostles ever catching any fish on their own?) They were jealous at times. Envious. They had temper tantrums, they pouted, they became obsessively depressed and fearful in times of trial. They ran in times of crisis, and they became proud of their status of being in the "in" group. They weren't too bright either, inasmuch as the meaning of a simple parable like the sower and the seed completely escaped them—so much so that they were forced to ask Jesus to explain it to them late at night. A parable that we consider within the intelligence of any fifth grader today was not comprehended by the men Jesus chose to be the leaders of His new Church.

Reading about the Apostles gave me a lot of courage. I could see that they didn't start out being perfect. It became clear to me that saints are not born but made. I thus learned that there is great hope for all of us. For when we ask, "What does God want with me?" there is a single, beautiful answer, an answer that can sometimes astonish us.

The answer is that <u>God wants us to become saints</u>.

God gave you and me everything we need to become saints: the strengths and the weaknesses, the happiness and the heartaches, the flaws and the ability to overcome them in absolutely heroic ways. Which is why, if you are mired in a particular sin or trapped by loneliness or depression, or simply restless and bored, you must sit up and pay attention to God's mission for you in this life.

God wants <u>you</u> to be a saint!

I do not say this to be dramatic, or to pep you up, or to discourage you, or for any other reason. I didn't make it up, and there are days I wish it weren't true. But it is true. The only tragedy in this life is not to have been a saint. The moment you come to grips with this great truth, your life will change forever into one extraordinary journey toward holiness.

YES, YOU!

Whenever I discuss the possibility of sainthood for each and every one of us, people start shaking their heads. Like me forty years ago, they think of the saints as statues, lovely romanticized men and women who always have a faraway look in their eyes. They get caught up in the halos and the visions. They look into their closets and they don't see any long robes or flowing tunics. They look into their daily lives and they don't see any burning stakes or persecutors. Somehow, life at 1001 Pleasant Lane, however pleasant or unpleasant it may be, just doesn't seem like the proper stage for a bona fide saint.

But it's not only the trappings of sainthood that make it seem so distant to us. The raw materials, like our hearts and minds and souls, also seem to present a problem. People cling to false notions of their own mediocrity, as if avoiding sanctity is somehow a safer, more comfortable existence. They'd rather do just enough to get by. It's as if they're aiming for Purgatory. "I'm not good enough," they insist, or "I'm not gentle enough," or "I'm just not cut out for that sort of thing."

Applesauce! God is looking for sinners and weaklings and everyday people just like you and me. Just because we live in suburbia or drink diet colas or worry about the Joneses doesn't mean we can't be saints. Housewives and executives and plumbers and waitresses can become saints. After all, Saint Matthew was a tax collector! And Saint Paul, before he made his "career change," was a persecutor of Christians. Throughout history, the saints have come from all economic classes and all walks of life. In many cases, they have been guilty of sins that make you and me look like real light-weights. Often they have been faced with struggles for sanctity that lasted their entire lifetimes.

But what did each of these amazing human beings have in common? What was it, in the end, that forged them into images of God Himself: loving, virtuous, and deeply holy? Why was God able to work wonders through these people rather than through others?

The answer is very simple. Saints are, if you'll pardon my theological shorthand, God's "dummies" and "dodos." "Oh, c'mon, Mother!" you say. "Saint Thomas Aquinas a dummy? What can you possibly mean?" What I mean is that in the spiritual life God has a special love for those who are willing to be fools for His Love, for those who have the courage to plunge forward full steam ahead when it comes to serving Him. I'm not saying that "dummies" are stupid. In fact, some of my most brilliant friends are dummies. Dummies are simply people who don't know that it can't be done. They only understand that they've got to be tough, that they've got to be humble, that they've got to trust absolutely in the Lord. And they know that if they do all these things— if they just try to do all these things—and if they do them in the Name of the Father, and of the Son, and of the Holy Spirit, then they are sure to please the Lord and bring forth blessings for the entire world.

And that is what God wants with us.

DOING THE RIDICULOUS

Maybe being one of the Lord's "dummies" is not what you had in mind. But what's so great about what you're doing right now? No offense, but constantly watching soap operas or televised football games isn't exactly going to get you into Heaven. And I know that cruise was fun, but are vacations the big payoff in life? Is your job really the be-all and end-all of human existence? Not that there's anything wrong with enjoying your work or your recreation. It's only when they become your primary focus that you run into trouble.

God wants much more for you than a start-and-stop existence that depends on other people, other events, and other things for little crumbs of happiness. God wants you to achieve holiness. This is why being one of God's "dummies" is a way of life. It means uniting your will to God's Will in everything you do. To be able to decipher God's Will takes a bit of practice and some prudence, but we'll get to that a little later. First I want you to know that there is great joy in serving God and in uniting your will to His.

Sometimes uniting your will to God's Will leads you in a totally unexpected direction. Take, for example, how I got started in television. I'll never forget that first recording session back in 1978. After a brief search, we found a small production company where we could get studio time fairly inexpensively. We started one Saturday, with the nuns and a good friend, Jean Morris, plunking me down in a rocking chair. "Just start talking about God," they advised me. Right. Can you imagine how you'd feel if I aimed a camera at your face and said, "Okay, just start talking about God"? Well, I looked like Grandma Moses with an Andy Gump chin, and I sounded like Mickey Mouse. It was awful.

The nuns, however, prevailed over any second thoughts I was having, and we went back to try it again. And again. And again. Finally, we got a tape that we felt wouldn't embarrass the Lord. But there was just one problem. It was as if we were all dressed up with no place to go. We had forgotten that once you had a tape, you had to have a place to air it. Suddenly we were faced with a troubling question: Who'd want to air a tape of a cloistered nun talking about Scripture? The list, not surprisingly, was a short one. I asked Jean to hand-deliver the tape to the Christian Broadcasting Network in Virginia Beach, Virginia.

As it turned out, CBN had been looking for some Catholic programming, and when the program director called and said he wanted sixty more half-hour programs, it nearly knocked my shoes off. Without hesitation I said "No problem!" and turned to the nuns to rejoice. But after an impromptu party of cookies and fruit punch, we were hit by the horrible realization that the series would cost us over $25,000. Twenty-five thousand dollars! It was an enormous sum, and we couldn't imagine in our wildest dreams where we could get so much money.

But the Lord provided—through generous friends, willing volunteers, and encouraging well-wishers. The Lord opened many doors for us, although there were times when He closed them, too. Yet there was value even in the detours: sometimes it was necessary to wait for God to show us His Will before we could see the right direction to take. As long as we were willing to trust Him, even when lots of people told us that what we were doing was impractical, unreasonable, and impossible, the Lord took care of us.

And that is how we got into television. Many people, I suppose, would have been more cautious, more systematic, and more organized. They probably would have put together a budget, perhaps conducted a feasibility study, gathered a committee of professional planners, and decided—in about eighteen months—that the idea was basically untenable. This is where it pays to be a dummy. Because, in our own fashion, which rested largely on the power of prayer, we just did it. We didn't know that we couldn't do it; that didn't occur to us. All we knew was that it seemed, at that moment, that this was what God wanted. And during those months of trying to get EWTN on the air, I realized something very important about the ways of God.

There are times when, unless we are willing to do what seems humanly ridiculous, God will not do the miraculous.

Doing the ridiculous has become a sort of motto here at EWTN. When I say doing something "ridiculous," I don't mean acting in a foolhardy or reckless manner. Instead, I mean following the inspirations of the Lord and being willing to fail. We've undertaken many projects at EWTN; some succeeded, and some failed. But God asks that we be willing to take risks for His sake, and that we overcome our fear of failure. We've found that only through our willingness to take risks have we been able to proclaim His Word in ways that truly touch hearts. The network is tangible evidence of God's

51

Goodness at work, but it isn't the only way we serve Him—nor is it the only manifestation of His Goodness.

There are a lot of miracle stories at EWTN. But some of the most miraculous stories have come from viewers, callers, and other friends of the network. These people have seen God provide everything from reversals in terrible medical conditions to peaceful deaths and astonishing conversions. I am amazed at how many saints we have in our audience. There are so many who have perfectly united their wills to the Will of God, who are content with whatever He wants of them, who when they say in the Lord's Prayer "Thy Will be done" actually mean it. These are people who will probably never be canonized as saints. But that's not the point. The point is that they have achieved a holiness that teaches me, and everyone else whose lives they touch, about the Goodness of God.

Is it easy? Not at all. Indeed, holiness is hard work, because so much of the time we're at odds with ourselves. There are little voices in us that say, "It can't be done" or "I'm not good enough" or "I'm not strong enough" or "I'm not smart enough." But you see, God is good enough, strong enough, and smart enough to do anything. If you take holiness seriously, you will bend your will to His. You'll find a remarkable peace even in the midst of suffering, because you'll know that whatever is happening in your life is indeed the Will of God.

Being a dummy helps. But it's not just a matter of trusting God and being willing to take risks; it's not simply a question of jumping off some tall spiritual building. Honoring God's Will means fighting His battle against sin and evil. And the first place of combat is the battlefield of your own heart.

YOU'VE GOT TO OBEY

I'll never forget a little encounter I had back in Canton, Ohio. One of my first big projects as a nun was to build a grotto for the Blessed Mother. And, as usual, my assignment was to do it with no money. This meant that I had to canvas the community for donations. I wasn't very successful. I ended up calling the local pool hall looking for men with some "free time" to help me out.

Luckily, a fellow named Sam was there. I'd known him since I was a child. He was happy to volunteer the help of his friends. "Sure, Sister. Me and the boys'll be glad to take care of it for you." In an amazingly short time we had constructed a beautiful grotto, and in appreciation we buried a scroll that listed the names of the people who'd made it possible.

It was a few days before we were to have the grotto blessed. Sam and I were standing around admiring our work when he came up with the excellent suggestion that we plant some hemlock trees around the grotto.

"Great," I said. "But aren't they really expensive?"

"No problem," he replied. "There's a guy up the hill who's got a whole grove full of them. He'll never know if we pinch a few here and there."

"But Sam, that's stealing!" I insisted.

"No, it's not, Sister. Those trees belong to God, don't they?"

It's not often that I'm left with nothing to say. But Sam's response took me by surprise. I could tell that Sam's conscience needed a little enlightening. Yes, the trees belonged to God, but they also belonged to the man on whose property they grew. My friend Sam was a little fuzzy about what God required of him. In order to help me, he was willing to "suspend" the Commandment "Thou shalt not steal." He wasn't interested in seeking the truth; he was interested in obtaining the hemlocks.

Sam was deeply hurt when I refused his offer of the "free" trees. And I'm not sure he ever understood why it was wrong.

While most of us aren't inclined to pilfer hemlock trees, we often get trapped in a game of rationalizing whatever it is that we want to do. We change our ethics according to the situation we're in, instead of doing what we know to be right. This is where Scripture and the Church come in. We all need guidelines that are unchanging, truths we can live by. As a Catholic, I'm grateful for a Church that provides me with a clear understanding of what God wants from me. I respect the authority of the leaders of my Church, and I have made vows to obey God and the teachings of the Church.

But the need to obey is not confined to Catholics. All of us are called by God to obey His Commandments, and to respect those in authority. Now I realize that obedience is not a popular word today. But it is a critical element in living a holy life because, when we obey, we acknowledge that God has sovereign rights over us. He has the right to say what we can and cannot do.

I know that a lot of people balk at the word obedience. It sounds so repressive, as if I'm suggesting that we become passive or act like robots. But far from feeling restricted by my vow of obedience, I find great comfort in the realization that I'm not alone in my difficulties. The many "gray-area" decisions that present themselves every day are difficult enough in themselves without having to rely solely on my own limited knowledge. The Church's two thousand years of wisdom and experience back me up and help me to clarify what is right and wrong.

Obedience is not easy, and we're not always going to like it. But try we must. Our holiness comes from obedience to God's Laws, for His Laws are His Will made manifest. Obedience means sacrifice, sometimes extraordinary sacrifice. Most of us think of sacrifice as the act of giving up something, whether it is time, money, food, our own inclinations—whatever.

The true meaning of sacrifice, however, stems from its Latin root word, *sacer* (which means "holy"), as in *sacred*. The act of sacrifice makes you holy. When you diet, you don't give up food for its own sake but to achieve a more healthful body. When you take care of your family, you don't give up your freedom for its own sake but to achieve a more joyous home life. Sacrifice, in the spiritual sense, is not something you do for its own sake, but to become holy. The Church does not embody and administer God's Law for the sake of legislation, but because its mandate is to preserve the truth so that you can use it to know God and become a saint.

THE NEED TO REPENT

If you're just getting started in the spiritual life, you'll learn very quickly that obedience is a fine concept for the first ten minutes and then, before you know it, you've strayed. Nobody said this was going to be a bed of roses. For many people, it's a horrible shock to realize that as much as they want to obey God, love Him, and be like Him, they've got weaknesses that are going to foil attempt after attempt to do just that.

The lucky ones are aware of it. They know exactly the time and place where they've goofed up, they've been given the grace to know what they did was wrong, and—in the very best scenario—they have instantly asked God to forgive them. They have repented for their sins.

Repentance is critical to achieving holiness. Simply put, it means saying you're sorry to God—and meaning it. Anybody can look up at the sky and say, "Sorry, Lord." But getting to the point where you really know you've offended Him and really regret hurting Him takes a while. What makes it even more difficult is that 50 percent of the time we don't even know that we're hurting God. For one thing, the idea of hurting God seems odd; we wonder how we could possibly hurt Someone so powerful and wise, or how our puny actions could affect the Creator of the universe.

And yet they do. We all hurt God every day, because His Love for us, individually, is so strong. This is why it's so important to know that when we sin we are not simply making a mistake or doing something "bad." We are hurting Someone Who loves us very deeply. When we repent, we go to our wounded Lord and offer a truly sorry heart; we are sorry for our offense and we try never to repeat it.

Repentance means saying you're sorry, but it doesn't mean wallowing in guilt and shame or beating yourself up for committing this sin or that. Imagine three persons: a good person, a bad person, and a saint. All three fall into a big, juicy mud puddle, which represents sin.

What does the good person do? Well, the good person falls

55

in and thinks it's the very end of the universe. He can't believe he blew it. He looks at the mud all over him and he wonders how many people will notice it. He continues to sit there lamenting over it and feeling sorry for himself. And then, finally, he looks up to God and asks for forgiveness. "I'm sorry, Lord," he says. "I should have known better. I'm the lowest of the low. I hate myself. No punishment is too great for me." And on and on.

The bad person is equally predictable. He didn't fall into that mud puddle, he dived in head first. He sits there, and he loves it. He wallows in it, pouring the mud all over himself. He enjoys the mud.

But watch the saint now. The saint, remember, is not perfect, but he is holy. He will make mistakes. But his response is what sets him apart. For the saint falls into the mud puddle and instantly stands up, his eyes focused on God, asking for forgiveness immediately with a truly contrite heart. He doesn't dwell on the mistake by wringing his hands or by wondering what others will think of him or by focusing on himself. He turns to God with haste and humility, and he quickly moves on, determined never to make that mistake again.

When we fail to obey the Commandments, when we fall into sin or toy with temptation, our first inclination must be to repent. God in His Mercy will accept our plea for forgiveness. He will forgive us, and then we must move on. Obviously, God knows everything we do. He knows when we mightily overcome sin and He knows when we fall. The more we go to Him for forgiveness, the closer we will be to Him, and the more, as saints, we will become like Him.

YOU'VE GOT TO LOVE

There is a point in a saint's life when God is so apparent to him, when he loves God so much, that obedience and repentance become habits of life. It doesn't happen overnight. They tell me that bad habits take about two weeks to settle in, but I know that good habits take a lot longer. Love can move the whole process along, however. And when God's Love animates us, we are so powerfully moved that even the most selfish among us can act unselfishly, and even the most sinful among us can be repentant.

As you can guess, a love this powerful isn't what you find in those romance novels. What we're talking about here is the love of God, and if there is any secret to sanctity, it is this very love, this powerful, endless source of goodness. The love of God is important because it is eternal. As you exhaust your human love, God is there with the reserves, the love that enables you to respond with patience and compassion to the most tedious people and the most difficult situations in your life.

There is, I suppose, a shortcut to understanding and using that love, one that has always worked for me at least, and that is to try to see the people in my life as God might see them.

One afternoon, for example, an EWTN staff member was twenty minutes late in picking up a bishop at the airport—a nun's nightmare! At first, I looked at the poor girl with Angelica's eyes, which were at that moment teeming with fire. But then I stopped myself and tried to see the girl with God's eyes and to be patient, loving, and forgiving. God required that I give her the benefit of the doubt and listen to the reason why she was late. While Angelica could only see error or incompetence and didn't want to hear any excuses, God knew that she had been given the wrong flight information. God understood that she was not at fault; but He also knew that twenty minutes in the scheme of eternity just wasn't a lot of time to worry about. Even more probable, God might have had someone at the airport for the bishop to minister to, or He might have wanted the bishop to have a few moments of peace and meditation, and those twenty minutes might have been put to beautiful use.

In God's world, there is much more than meets the eye, and it is in adjusting to His Vision that we can learn to love as He loves. As an Italian with a short fuse, I can tell you that while all this may sound palatable on paper, it is, in practice, no picnic. For you and I both have in our lives some people whom we find it pretty hard to love.

I think one of the great barriers to loving, truly loving, as God loves is that we are all tempted to judge the person we're trying to love. This is a problem especially when the object of our love has hurt us in some way, whether it was a betrayal, a broken promise, or a disappointment. We tend to forget that we're not exactly perfect specimens of the best human behavior, and were it not for the grace of God we might have been the offending party ourselves. It's not easy to come up with a loving response to a husband who's been running around or a wife who's been gambling away the family money or a child who uses his parents continually, leans on them too much, or is forever trying to make them feel guilty about not loving him enough! But if we can refrain from judging our loved ones too much—and if we can try to see them through the eyes of God—we will find strength and resource in God's endless love to endure what cannot be changed.

I am reminded of a woman named Marie, a deeply spiritual friend of ours, who once shared an insight she had about her estranged brother.

"He was in terrible shape, Mother," she told me in my office one afternoon. "He would start his day with Bloody Marys, then have the traditional three-martini lunch, and finally unwind from his long day of drinking at the local bar. I don't know how he did it, but he kept up an almost presentable front to the outside world. Only his wife and family knew what was going on, and we were all beside ourselves with worry and anger.

"Well, this was my brother, and for some reason I took his weakness personally. I really resented it. I resented the fact that so much had been given him—a beautiful upbringing and family—and that he had chosen to make a mockery of it. I couldn't accept that he might have a heartache or need. I just looked at him as lower than myself, as someone who was enjoying overindulgence.

"So I prayed. One morning I asked God to give me the patience or the wisdom or whatever I needed to love my brother and to help him. I met some friends for lunch and God showed me a little something about myself. As I was lighting up my fourth cigarette and asking the waitress for a third cup of coffee, I became acutely aware that I, too, was an addict. For some reason, I suppose because coffee and cigarettes are more socially acceptable, it had never occurred to me that I too might have a weakness for excess. It's crazy, isn't it, Mother. I'd spent years resenting my brother for a weakness of my own. Needless to say, it wasn't long before I was able to have some good talks with him and share some real compassion for what he was going through."

Marie had come to a very humbling and empowering understanding. I think a lot of us, like Marie, feel a kind of indignation about sins offensive to society like drinking and drugs, while never really examining our own excesses, like caffeine or overeating or complaining or gossiping. When we are given the light to know "Hey, I'm not perfect, either, and it's only by the grace of God that I'm not in that person's shoes," we grow in humility. We can be more compassionate. We can love as God loves, without judging others.

We all have weaknesses, and our knowledge of those weaknesses is vital if we are ever to achieve holiness. Knowing we're not perfect helps us to love others who aren't perfect; it gives us an important sense of humility and the power not to judge. Loving as God loves is the highest achievement of sainthood. It is what Christianity is all about.

For as you move forward on your spiritual journey, you will discover one very important thing: the Christian response to a daily life situation is not an easy response. It goes against our human nature to love someone who is hurting us, to obey laws that ask us to sacrifice, or to be patient and kind to strangers.

Christianity elevates our human nature by combining it with the supernatural. This combination enables us to respond to the trials and tribulations of everyday life. You can endure irritable children, a demanding spouse, a rude boss, and gossiping friends with your eyes set on a higher reality. You can rise above your human nature and unite your mind and your will to the Will of God. This is what sets saints apart. And as this slowly happens in your life and you come to fulfill the purpose God has set for you, an extraordinary transformation begins to take place.

PEOPLE WILL SEE GOD IN YOU

The first Christians were different from you and me. Whether they were in a marketplace or making a pilgrimage or hiding from their persecutors, everyone could tell that they were Christians, because they would share everything they had. They were compassionate, forgiving, gentle. I think that one of the great scandals in our time is that we do not radiate God's Love as they did two thousand years ago. An early Christian was known by his example. He didn't have to mention Our Lord's Name for anyone to be able to tell that he held God in his heart.

In a saint, you can see the love of God.

In the Gospel of Saint John, the Lord put it this way: "Make your home in Me, as I make Mine in you. As a branch cannot bear fruit all by itself, but must remain part of the vine, neither can you unless you remain in Me. I am the vine, you are the branches. Whoever remains in Me, with Me in him, bears fruit in plenty" (John 15:4–5).

Now what is Our Lord talking about when He says we will "bear fruit"? He is saying that we will bear signs of God's Love if only we will put our trust in Him. A heroic acceptance of suffering? Yes. Patience with an irritating person? Yes. Kindness to those who hurt us? Yes, that too.

This is why it is so important for us to seek and embrace God's Will for us.

A few years ago, I was called to visit a woman in a nearby hospital who was dying of bone cancer.

Suzanne was lying there in her private room, with a tired bouquet of daisies on her nightstand. She looked up when I came in and smiled an astonishing smile of peace and tranquility. "How are you, Suzanne?" I asked. "I'm fine, praise God," she replied.

Bone cancer, as you know, can cause an exceedingly painful and debilitating death. As we visited some more, I learned that Suzanne's husband had walked out on her when she was first diagnosed as having cancer. Earlier that very afternoon, she had signed papers that gave custody of her daughter, all she had left in the world, to her sister.

It was a humbling experience for me. As I walked down the hospital corridor, nurses and doctors ran up to greet me and to ask for prayers and support, thinking I was a person of faith and devotion. But there was enough faith and devotion in the sweet smile of Suzanne on her deathbed to shame me and the world forever. She showed no bitterness and not a trace of anger. She radiated a convincing knowledge that no matter what her sorrow and pain, somehow God would bring good out of her tragic end. Her witness made an incredible impact on me, because the moment I looked into her eyes I knew I was seeing Jesus.

If you are bearing good fruit, your neighbor will be able to read the Gospel in your life, even if he's never read Scripture or thinks little of religion or God. He will know that there is something about you that is different, even if he does not know that "something" is God. Nothing gives us more courage than to see an imperfect, bungling person striving to be holy. And it is these selfsame, bungling individuals that God calls to be saints.

THE JOURNEY TO HOLINESS

Recently we were celebrating a nun's birthday, and I noticed that amidst the chatter and song there was one nun who was sitting alone, looking rather thoughtful.

"Too much excitement for you, Sister?" I asked teasingly as I sat down next to her.

"No, Mother," she said with a smile. "I was just counting the number of opportunities the Lord gave me to be holy today."

Every day we get new opportunities to trust in God's Providence and to radiate His Love. What makes the spiritual journey different from any other is that when we're not moving forward, we're falling back. It's never a matter of saying, "Okay, now I'm going to love God" and then taking a few days off to coast. Loving God is not an on-again, off-again proposition. It is a continuing journey. And it matters more than anything else in your life. To advance on this journey, you have to be committed to a life of holiness.

We all grow in holiness in different ways; each one of us has a unique path. But as unique as each path is, I think we all pass by the same signposts.

- We must respect and obey the laws of God.
- We must repent for our sins and ask for God's forgiveness with a sincere heart.
- We must love as God loves.
- We must radiate God's goodness.

There is so much that God wants you to accomplish, so much you can accomplish for Him. Knowing that God is present, operating in your life every moment of every day, you can move forward without fear, with the courage of the saints, to fulfill the special mission He has in mind for you.

You may be the only Jesus your neighbor will ever see. You may be the only example of mercy and compassion that a co-worker will ever know. Your courage may be the only sign of holiness a fellow patient will ever encounter. Your patience in your marriage may be the only witness of God's strength and of supernatural fortitude that your friends may ever witness.

God has something very special in mind for you.
He wants you to be a saint.

—3—

Why Do We Suffer?

A FEW YEARS AGO, a warm and gracious woman with amazingly big eyes, and an even bigger heart, walked into the monastery. "Mother Angelica, please," she said to the nun on duty. As usual, we were in the throes of a major crisis, so it was about thirty minutes before I walked out to greet one of the most loving, genuine people I have ever met. "Mother, my name is Rosalie Jones, and I've got suffering on my mind," she said with a grin on her face. Small world, I thought to myself, and ushered her in.

"So what's troubling you, Rosalie?" I said as we sat down, ready to listen to an account of personal tragedy or family crisis.

"It's just this," she said. "My brother is the pastor of our church. For the past five years he and I have had a running argument about suffering, and I figured it was high time somebody like you settled it. He says that suffering happens only because of sin. He says that it's a lightning bolt from Heaven telling us we'd best shape up.

"But Mother, I firmly believe that we suffer for a reason,

and that reason is to be like Jesus. It seems to me that when the Lord gives you tribulations, He expects you to tribulate.''

Well, as you can guess, I was enchanted. Rosalie and I talked for about twenty minutes, and when we'd finished I was more refreshed and inspired than I'd been in a long time. It was no coincidence that Rosalie had walked into our monastery on the morning of one of our biggest crises. After she left, I burst in on the nuns and told them, ''Sisters, it's time to tribulate!''

I think a big problem in this country is that so many people suffer without understanding why, as if everything were some cosmic accident. None of us really knows how to ''tribulate'' and yet our lives are filled with tribulation. And suffering is a very democratic experience. Nobody can completely escape illness or injury. All the money in the world can't save a dying marriage or solve a spiritual conflict. Life isn't easy, and we who have so much here in America have a hard time accepting that.

If you are asking ''Why do we suffer?'' I can presume that this is a difficult time for you. Maybe the past few years have been tough, or maybe your life has been turned upside down by a recent event. I can't change the way you feel, but I can help to change the way you think. And this new way of thinking will help you to clarify what is happening in your life—and why.

You know, God gave us extraordinary minds, but we rarely use them to work through the nitty-gritty of daily life. We don't need a Ph.D. to know that God exists. But we do need a brand of spiritual smarts, and that is what we're going to work on now. So many of us skim along the surface of life without questioning much, until something really jolts us. Usually it's a tragedy. Sometimes it's the horrible realization that we've been stuck in a bad situation for years. Suddenly we can't take it anymore and we become trapped in our grief or self-pity. We want to change it. We want to be convinced that there is a reason for all of the madness, all of the pain, all of the tedium in our lives and all of the heartache all around us.

We want to be sure that, somehow, it all makes sense.

BARKING UP THE WRONG TREE

If you look to the world to answer the question of why we suffer, you will come up empty-handed. The world cannot tell you why we suffer. This is why most of us are content to stew about in self-pity or punch our fists through walls or bend our neighbor's ear all day long about this ailment and that. As a group, we don't handle suffering very well.

Most of the time we try to lay blame. "My wife drove me to drink." "My son stuck me in this nursing home." "My co-worker got me fired." "I was born too late." I've even heard people blame Adam and Eve for their miseries!

Now if you listen closely to all these excuses, you'll hear a lot about other people, society, history, and the devil, but not one word about God. This is where we make our mistake. And it's a biggie. Because if we really want the truth, we can't refuse to face it for what it is. If we try to dodge the reality of suffering, we lose sight of one of the most elemental and powerful truths of our faith: that it is God Himself Who permits it.

THE MYSTERY

God permits all suffering.

He loves you so much that He knows every tear you have ever shed. Yet He has also allowed the things to happen that caused you to shed them. Does this mean that God does not love you in a deep and personal way? Not at all. Does this mean that God is insensitive or mad at you or vengeful? We know this cannot be true. God doesn't sit on His Throne and arbitrarily dictate, "I want a landslide in Wyoming" or "Give Jim Bell lung cancer this morning" or "Make sure Mary Evans loses a lot of sleep tonight."

But each and every day our Omnipotent God, Who controls all things, does permit suffering to take place in our lives. He does this because He wants more for you than a shallow and untested existence. He doesn't just want to be a shelter you run to every time you're in need. His Will is that you be perfected. In the process of perfection it is necessary that He sometimes allow you to suffer extraordinary pain and difficulty.

God manifests His Will in two ways: by either ordaining or permitting whatever is happening to us in the present moment. His Ordaining Will is His perfect Will. He ordained that you would be born. He did so with all of His Imagination and Intelligence and Power because He loved the idea of you. But throughout your life millions of factors—the actions of other people, outside circumstances, economics, nature, the opposing will of Satan—will expose you to countless possibilities. These possibilities, which can include your own pain and heartache, are permitted by God.

Often we pray to the Father when we want Him to change something in our lives. But God's Permitting Will sees beyond the present moment in which we live to the bounds of eternity. If things don't change, it is because He understands far more than we ever will the necessity of our living through that situation.

Souls are shaped not only by laughter and ease but also by pain and trial. It is your soul that God treasures. He treasures your soul more than you do. He knows that our losses in this world help to shape our souls for the next. He knows that the grief you have in your heart will pass. He knows that whatever it is you are experiencing now will be brought to a higher good.

This is why, as difficult or preposterous as it may sound, we must try to understand that in a profound way suffering is a gift from God.

OUR SUFFERING IS A GIFT

God permits our suffering because it has a purpose. I know this is hard to accept. It takes time, sometimes it takes years, to truly grasp any good in what might now be a terrible sorrow for you.

If you have ever watched my television show, you might have noticed that I wear a metal brace on my left leg. I won't beat around the bush. My leg and my back give me constant, wearying pain. You'd think that after some thirty-odd years I'd get used to it. But I haven't. And yet, I thank God every day for the very pain that sometimes drains me of all my energy.

You're probably thinking, "Isn't that a bit much?"

Yes, it is, except that as a contemplative nun I've been called to a life of prayer. Over the years as I've prayed about my pain, which can sometimes be so severe as to make me cry out to God for relief, a strange feeling has come to me, a feeling of being drawn closer to God, of being pulled out of myself and my imperfect body into another dimension. In this dimension there is peace.

Could I have reached it without all these years of pain? I'll never know. Perhaps other people reach it just by kneeling down in a pew on a Sunday morning or staring up at a starlit sky. But this dimension only opened up to me after I had passed through all the barriers of pain, and if those barriers had not existed, I don't know if I would have ever made the effort that has been required to discover it.

Yes, I am thankful for the pain, but that doesn't mean I expect that tonight you'll be thanking God for your divorce or that you'll be praising Him for your high blood pressure. It takes time to truly grasp any good in what might now be a terrible sorrow for you.

Even though it won't relieve your pain right now, there is one thing you can do that will change the nature of your pain and how it affects your life.

You can trust God.

IN GOD WE TRUST

Most of us, if pressed, would say that we trust in God; we say so even on our currency. But trusting in God in those black hours when everything seems to be slipping through your fingers isn't easy. In those moments, you have probably found that trust in God is as elusive as the contentment you seek.

The fact is that we cannot truly trust in God without the aid of our spiritual companions, Faith, Hope, and Love. If you are suffering right now, your most powerful plea to God should be for an increase in these theological virtues. You need the help of these virtues to truly grasp that God is guiding you through all of this, no matter how much it hurts. You need the humility to know that our minds are limited, and that in the Mind of God there is a vastness that we cannot begin to fathom. Indeed, between God's Wisdom and our wisdom there is an awesome distance. But as we come to trust God's Wisdom, we can find peace, even joy, in our suffering.

I'm not going to take away your pain, because I can't. However, I can help you to understand your pain, by first addressing the reality of it and then by helping you to discern God's action in it.

But we must begin with an important understanding. We must understand fully that we live in a completely ordered existence in which all forces, good and evil, are ultimately permitted by God. God eventually brings good out of whatever happens in this life. He knows what you are going through at this moment and He is there to give you what you need to get through it. As hard as it is to comprehend, you must realize that God loves you more than you love yourself. And realizing that He loves you that much, you can accept, with confidence, that there is a purpose, a holy, exalted purpose, in all things that He ordains or permits.

So we can see that simply wishing away our pain and sadness runs counter to God's Will. The positive thinkers who try to cheer us out of our depression, who tell us we're okay when we're not, lead us very badly astray. They make us feel that there is some sort of happy button we can punch to make everything in life all right. They imply that life is just a matter of a good attitude, that we should be able to merrily jump out of bed every morning with a big grin on our face, ready to tackle the day, even if we've lost our job, disappointed our family, or just found out we have a deadly disease.

Well, I don't know about you, but even on a good day when my alarm goes off I'm not excited, I'm tired. I feel like a thousand pounds of dead weight. If I saw someone with a big grin on her face at 5 a.m., I would rush her to the doctor. So let's start by stating clearly this basic assumption: it's "okay" to suffer. It's "okay" to feel pain.

But it is not "okay" to pretend that your pain and suffering don't exist, because your pain and suffering have a purpose. I'm not saying you should dwell upon suffering or make a career out of it, but that you should grow stronger and more holy in it. As Christians, we are called to resemble Jesus. Jesus did not shrug off His Suffering; He did not pretend that everything was all right when the world was jeering at Him. Nor did He question the Father's motives in allowing Him to experience that humiliation. Jesus was a realist, a holy realist, Who knew that God permitted His Suffering for a higher purpose. Jesus did not deny His Suffering, because He knew it was willed by God.

THE CHRISTIAN RESPONSE

No matter what the cause of your suffering, no matter what circumstances have brought you to this point in your life, God waits for your response.

Even now, events may seem to have the better of you. Will you let them disable you? Will you allow them to paralyze you so that you can't move, or act, or laugh again? Of course not. God wants you to grow strong in your suffering. He wants you to become holy.

"But how can I grow strong when my eyes are so swollen

from crying that I can't even see?'' you ask. Or "How can I grow holy when I'm so lonely and depressed that I can barely make it through the day?''

You can look at the example of Jesus.

Indeed, if we take each situation, no matter how trying, and respond to it as Jesus would, we are going to experience a tremendous peace. Will it be easy? Absolutely not. As a matter of fact, the Christian response often runs counter to everything in our nature. This is why we should pay particular attention to the Gospels, for they give us in Jesus' life the ultimate ''how-to'' for every situation.

To be a Christian is to follow the example of Jesus. When you are mourning the death of a loved one, you are like Jesus weeping for Lazarus. When you are accused unjustly, you are like Jesus standing before Pilate. When you forgive an enemy, you are like Jesus on the Cross.

God has allowed you to suffer so that you can be molded into the Image of His Son. This is the purpose of suffering in your life. If you accept Him, you must accept His Suffering. And it is the manner in which you accept your suffering that will make you holy.

I know it's hard. It was hard for Him, too.

A couple of years ago, the network was really going downhill financially. Our creditors were threatening to close us down. I had a lot of pain. We were getting flak from everywhere, even from people who were supposed to be our friends. I had had it. As you know, I am a cloistered nun, and my first vocation is the Perpetual Adoration of Jesus in the Blessed Sacrament (the Holy Eucharist). All the nuns and I keep a constant vigil before the Lord in our chapel here at the monastery. We are contemplatives, which means that we serve God through prayer and meditation.

The reason I explain all this is that when God started moving us into the satellite television business, it required a lot of trust and abandonment to His Will. It was not easy. But when it looked like the whole thing was going to pieces, I responded with anger. I was mad. I remember storming into the chapel one morning. I looked up at the Blessed Sacrament and said, "Today is not the day for problems, Lord. I've got a lot of pain and I can't take any more."

I was silent for a while. The Lord was, too.

"Why me, Lord?" I finally cried out. "Why me?"

Then I just stared at Him. My eyes were fixed on the Holy Eucharist as if to say, "Well, answer me!"

There was a strange silence.

Then, after a few moments, a gentle Voice answered.

"Yes, Angelica," He said. "And why Me?"

Well, needless to say, I felt like a worm, and immediately I knelt down and wept and said, "Lord, please erase that tape. It's okay. I didn't mean it. If You want us to keep going with this network, we'll take the whole blooming mess." I asked Him to forgive me and I never brought it up again. We've had better days since that morning, and worse days. And the only reason I mention it now is because I think you, too, might be wondering, "Why me?"

Accepting our trials and pain and suffering with grace is the hardest thing in life. Knowing that God is with you every moment and bringing good out of it all takes a constant infusion of Faith, Hope, and Love. Following in Jesus' Footsteps is not easy; it's the hardest path you can take. But that path leads to holiness. And holiness leads to God. And this is why—as difficult and confounding and demanding as it is—we must muster our courage in suffering.

Each of us has a unique path to holiness. But over our lifetimes, there are certain kinds of suffering that all of us, in different ways, could come to experience. These different kinds of suffering are worth exploring, for in each we will be able to see the good that God brings from our pain and uncertainty.

Let's look at some of the most broadly experienced kinds of suffering in this life.

PREVENTIVE SUFFERING

The first kind of suffering, preventive, is in many ways the most interesting. This is when God permits a momentary setback or delay or even a painful period in your life because He has, down the road, something much better in mind for you.

For example, you probably know some people who spent their younger days unhappily single, only to meet Mister or Miss Right one day and dash off into matrimonial bliss. The loneliness and the defeats they suffered for so many years melted away the moment they met their true partner.

This is preventive suffering. God prevented them from making a choice that they would not have been able to live with, because He knew there was someone better down the road. Preventive suffering takes many forms, of course, and sometimes God's work is not so obvious. But in this area of suffering, God assumes the very traditional role of Father.

When we were growing up, we might have resented it when our parents forbade us to go to a dance or refused to let us drink wine with the adults at the dinner table. At the time, we probably thought that life was one injustice after another, and that our parents were dictators. In a funny way, we act like the same impatient children when God permits us to suffer a temporary setback or an inconvenience of some sort. We don't think for a minute that there might be a reason, a very good reason, for all that we suffer at the moment.

I recently met a wonderful young man in Florida; he was working with the newborn children of drug-addicted mothers, mostly cocaine users. Kevin couldn't have been more than twenty-four years old. He told me that he had spent almost two years job-hunting after he graduated from an Ivy League school. He had gone to forty interviews, and for some reason every one of them was a disaster. He would get lost going to an interview, show up on the wrong day, or get tongue-tied. One day he was inexplicably rude to the vice president of a major brokerage house.

Kevin's behavior confused even Kevin. He had not been

72

what you would call a problem child. He was an honor student, an outgoing, lovable young Irishman, and here he was blowing every single interview. At first he tried to laugh it off. Then he started to think he was "jinxed." "Here I was, the guy the family had pinned their hopes on, and at twenty-one I was a loser. I was broke and depressed and my self-esteem was at rock bottom. Even my mother lost faith in me. She booted me out of the house with a twenty-dollar bill and a pat on the back. I hitchhiked to Florida and ended up in this hospital cafeteria, looking for a cheap meal. I never left."

Kevin is not an especially religious person, but he acknowledges that it was no accident that got him into the business of caring for drug-dependent mothers and their infants. "It's weird. I'm almost starting to think it was God Who allowed me to make a fool of myself on Wall Street. But this is obviously where I belong," he said to me on his way to the nursery. "I mean, could you see me in a brokerage house?" he asked, holding up a four-day-old infant in his arms. I couldn't see him trading securities. But I could see that Wall Street's loss was God's gain.

It takes Faith, Hope, and Love to realize that even while we suffer, God is leading us to better things. Kevin calls it "weird." Others call it chance. But Christians realize that it is God. This knowledge does not take away the pain, but allows us to persevere with courage and even joy in the midst of our sorrow.

Preventive suffering is an occasion to grow in your faith. Your holiness will come from doing what you can to change the situation, and accepting what you cannot change with joy and conviction.

CORRECTIVE SUFFERING

You're not going to like this one. Nobody does. But there is such a thing as corrective suffering, and by that I mean just what you hope I don't mean. In the Book of Revelation, the Messiah says: "I am the One Who reproves and disciplines all those He loves'' (Revelation 3:19). Now I realize that the minute you read this all your alarms go off, because you don't like to think of a Supreme Being picking on mere mortals. But our God is a great God. He doesn't need to pick on anyone. So when He does correct us, it is out of love and justice. It is not because He doesn't care, but because He cares very much.

Corrective suffering works very powerfully in our souls. I know a media executive in New York City who experienced some terrible financial setbacks a couple of years ago. His company was on a yo-yo, and every time it looked like he had come up with a brilliant recovery plan, a bizarre turn of events would undo everything. He wrote:

> *"I was starting to panic because everything was going sour. I'm pretty good at what I do—at least I thought I was—but for a while it seemed that the whole world was against me.*
>
> *"One day I went into Saint Patrick's Cathedral, my home away from home. I was only there for a few minutes, and I asked Saint Patrick to intervene for me and my company. He responded distinctly. 'For your little troubles pray directly to God. I've got more important things than your company's finances to pray about. Because now and forever I am praying for your immortal soul.'*
>
> *"This is not exactly what a man at the end of his rope wants to hear, but it changed my life. I realized that God had allowed these events so I could regain my perspective on what's important in life. The year 1985 was the worst of my life financially—we're still recovering—but I thank God every day for it."*

Corrective suffering is more difficult than all other kinds of suffering. But remember, God knows exactly what the outcome will be. God knew that the hotshot media executive would grow light-years in holiness if he could acknowledge his dependence on God. This was a correction born of a deep and personal love, the kind that caused Saint Teresa of Avila to say: "Lord, if this is how You treat your friends, no wonder You have so few of them." But there are also corrections born of God's Justice, and sometimes, with our limited knowledge, these are pretty hard to handle.

Jean, a sixty-seven-year-old widow from Texas, called the network one night from her hospital room, where she was watching EWTN on closed-circuit television. She was dying of lung cancer. "Mother, I smoked three packs of cigarettes a day almost all my life, even after I learned it was deadly," she said in her deep Texas drawl. "My life was an act of defiance from the word 'go.' At first I wanted to torment my mother. Then I wanted to annoy my husband, whom I resented for reasons I still can't figure out, since he was so loving and kind. Now I'm paying for it and let me tell you, I couldn't be happier.

"God is letting me clear up my debt for all of the wrongmindedness in my life. I figure that as long as I give God the last word and accept this lung cancer as a gift of some kind, I will have peace. God gave me a chance to settle up. He didn't have to do that. I just hope I can live up to the kind of dying He gave me to do."

When Jean died three weeks later, we got a note from one of her daughters. The daughter wrote that Jean looked oddly youthful in her final days, and radiated an unusual calm and serenity. "It was as if the rebelliousness of her whole life had been lifted from her so she could die a happy woman."

God, because He is God, is interested in one thing: your soul. Corrective suffering addresses the needs of our souls, whether we are too attached to this world like the media executive or whether, like Jean, we must be purged of our hatred before moving on to the next world. Corrective suffering is not a matter of cheating on your income taxes one day and getting struck by lightning the next. It is far more serious, and much more subtle.

In his Letter to the Hebrews, Saint Paul says: "When the Lord corrects you, do not treat it lightly; but do not get discouraged when He reprimands you" (Hebrews 12:5). You must realize that there will be some tragedies and disappointments in your life that will be used to purify you. You must accept the fact that life is not all fun and games. I never got a reprimand that was nice and flowery, or a correction that didn't cause pain. As you move along on your spiritual journey, you will understand that the reason for this pain and suffering is to keep you dependent, to keep you close to God. "For the Lord trains the ones that He loves and He punishes all those that He acknowledges as His sons" (Hebrews 12:6).

REPENTANT SUFFERING

Sometimes God allows us to experience the trauma and pain brought on by our sinful choices so that we may be humbled and therefore closer to Him. I call this repentant suffering.

For example, if a woman chooses to have an affair and becomes pregnant, the inevitable suffering she endures is a direct result of that action which violated one of the Ten Commandments of God. Particularly if the man abandons her, she might well believe that she is unlucky in love, that she always attracts the wrong sort of person, that men are always taking advantage of her. Yet she fails to recognize that her pain is caused by her own sinful choice. The affair has made disorder out of God's order, and the natural consequence of this sin is guilt and unhappiness.

Please understand what I'm trying to say, because the point is critical. Many times today the unborn child is considered the sin. People mistakenly believe that the "tragedy" is the fact that the woman "got caught" with an unexpected pregnancy. They believe her action is wrong because she was irresponsible and she didn't "protect" herself from this horrible development.

But the emphasis is badly misplaced. The baby is not the sin. The affair is the sin. And the affair would be sinful whether or not the woman conceived a child.

What the woman needs to do is to receive the Sacrament of Reconciliation (go to Confession) if she is Catholic, say to the Lord "I'm sorry," and ask Him to help her persevere through this difficult time. We must know that when we repent, God is near to comfort, guide, and lead us to great holiness. We have to understand that things may not necessarily change. But our ability to endure them, knowing that God will bear great fruit in our souls, will certainly lighten the burden.

It is at this moment that the woman can respond to God's forgiveness and grow closer to Him than she ever dreamed possible. She is now faced with the terrifying decision of what to do about her baby. With God's grace, she can obtain the courage to resist aborting the child, even if it means she would have to raise the child by herself or give the baby up for adoption. For abortion would simply be a continuation of the sin, a compounding of the original offense against God, opening the floodgates to a lifetime of guilt and regret.

Lest you think that I've forgotten the remaining party in this situation, I want to discuss the man who participated in the affair. While it may seem that he has resolved the situation for himself by abandoning the woman, this is not at all the case. In fact, the man is far more culpable before God, not only for his involvement in the affair but also for his refusal to accept responsibility for the child. Unless the man confronts his sin and asks God's forgiveness, he remains separated from God.

Another example of repentant suffering is the suffering of Saint Paul. As you know—and as he likes to remind us—Saint Paul was a persecutor of Christians before his conversion. He bragged about capturing Christians and bringing them before the authorities for exile or execution. On his way to Damascus he was suddenly struck from his horse, saw a bright light, and heard a Voice that said, "Saul, Saul, why do you persecute Me?" From this moment Saul was blind, and he only regained his sight after a Christian named Ananias prayed for him.

Saul, from then on known as Paul, never forgot what he had done. His repentance was something that carried him through the rest of his life. If you have made wrongful choices, the result of your sinfulness may very well be suffering. If you will recognize your sin, admit it to God (for

Catholics through Confession), and ask forgiveness, good will be brought from your suffering. We may live with the consequences of our own actions for years to come. But even in these trying circumstances, we can be at peace with God through repentance.

I have real admiration for those individuals who with God's grace have used their mistakes to help others. Members of groups such as Alcoholics Anonymous, Women Exploited by Abortion, and many drug rehabilitation organizations have shared their struggle and repentance with others to try to keep them from making the same mistakes. Their continuing efforts demonstrate the Mercy of God while adding to their own holiness.

REDEMPTIVE SUFFERING

One night an elderly woman called the live show and in a thin, frail voice asked a very tough question. "Mother," she said, "I am a seventy-eight-year-old widow, and I'm nearly blind. I can barely get around at this point, and each day gets worse. All day long I pray for the Church and for Pope John Paul II, but that's just about all I do. I don't even eat decent meals. Is it all right to pray to God for relief from my suffering?"

Silence. I had to think about this one for a moment, since my answer was "Yes." We can and should pray for relief from our suffering; we should pray for anything we need from our Father in Heaven, because He is always so glad to hear from us. As long as we are united to His "Nos" as well as His "Yeses," we can ask for anything. But here, with this woman, God was doing an amazing thing.

This woman was quietly courageous in her suffering, peaceful and accepting. She had devoted her remaining strength to daily prayer for the Church, which always needs our prayers, and her suffering as a result had a very redemptive quality to it. Her vision had failed, but her prayers were helping others to see. I told her it was all right to pray for her suffering to be eased, but to know that she was already closer to God than most of us ever even strive to be. I asked her to pray for the network and I thanked God for letting this extraordinary woman stay with us, if only for a little while longer.

Saint Paul says, "This may be a wicked age, but your lives should redeem it" (Ephesians 5:16). The word "redeem" means to rescue, to free, to pay the penalty incurred by another. We often lose sight of the definition "to set free" and we overlook the opportunities we have to suffer on behalf of others. When we see a woman like this, who is weak and without her sight, we take courage. When we see a Christian turn to God even when he is filled with sorrow, we hope. When a friend who has suffered a terrible tragedy can begin again in trust and love, we find strength to go on with our own journey.

SUFFERING AS WITNESS

Sometimes, if we are fortunate, God may put in our path a very special person. A person who is so serene, so quietly confident in God that we must stop for a moment to fully grasp that person's goodness. Usually, we can only read about characters like this or see them in movies or on television, because—most of the time—these people are almost too good to be true. Life clobbers them and they fight back with dignity. Although they may have moments of question and doubt, they never lose faith. They seldom lose hope. And they never stop loving. For Christians, these people are real heroes.

One night I had the honor of hosting such a woman on our call-in program. Gail is the mother of a beautiful little girl, Joya, who is mentally retarded. Gail sees the miracle in every word Joya speaks, in every task that she accomplishes.

According to Gail, she didn't wake up one morning with unshakable peace over her daughter's handicap. Instead, Gail went through long nights of anguish and anger. Her marriage fell apart while the demands of caring for a special child like

Joya grew more pressing. But Gail thanks God every day for the gift of Joya. And she is the first one to say that having Joya has given her a joy that she had never known before, a joy that no one can take away.

Now on first inspection, you might say that this woman was just a passive sort of character, a woman who simply resigned herself to the inevitable. Some might say she was not facing reality. Most of us might wonder how a woman like this could put up with such suffering—and still call God "good" for His gift of Joya to her.

The answer is that God trusts this woman more than He trusts most of us. We always think of having faith in God, but we never consider that God might put some faith in us. A woman who has been deserted and left to raise her handicapped child alone—and who still loves God with a full heart—is one of the most powerful witnesses to the reality of another world. If a smiling couple with perfect children and a happy home say "God is good," we might be unimpressed. But if a woman who has been given a heavy cross to bear says "God is good," we are inspired.

Some of you might be thinking to yourselves, "Uh-oh, I sure hope God isn't going to make me a witness." But God will never give you more than you can handle. He will never give you more suffering or heartache or pain than you can survive: "You can trust God not to try you beyond your strength" (1 Corinthians 10:13). God obviously knew that Gail could speak loudly and forcefully to the beauty of His Love. And in doing so, this humble woman resembles Jesus, the One Whom God loves most.

PERSONAL SUFFERING

Personal suffering can cause us the most pain of all, but it can also be the most sanctifying and enlightening. It tells us what our faults are and where we are weak. If you look into your own life, you can see that selfishness can destroy relationships, families, and even souls. If you are embroiled in some kind of personal suffering, you must ask yourself honestly if this is something of your own making or if it is a matter of temperament that you'll just have to work on.

Sometimes we bring personal suffering upon ourselves. A lady from Arizona was in our studio audience recently and asked me to speak with her after the show. "I've been grieving over my two daughters and I don't know where to turn," she confided. "They've been feuding bitterly and haven't spoken to each other for two years. They're dividing up the entire family over their differences."

"What started the feud?" I asked cautiously, imagining all sorts of terrible possibilities.

"The commode," she answered.

"Er, the commode?" I said. "A, uh '<u>commode</u>' commode?"

"Why, yes, but this one is beautifully inlaid with gold."

"Now I want to make sure I've got this straight," I said, looking at her with a bit of disbelief. "We are talking about a toilet, right?"

"Yes, Mother, I suppose you could call it a toilet. But we call it a commode, and this commode is an antique. Each girl claims her grandmother promised it to her."

I could hardly believe my ears.

My response was brief. "You go home and tell those girls that Mother Angelica said they should take turns sticking their heads in that ridiculous toilet!"

This story is an example of suffering that came from pettiness and greed. But in many cases, personal suffering comes to us because of our personalities and our temperaments. The sensitive person who can't take a word of criticism is an example. Or the harsh person who always condemns others and then regrets it later. The vengeful person who is consumed in "getting even" also bears this kind of cross.

You can identify that it is a situation of your own making when:

- You won't forgive someone because you are proud and stubborn, so you are making life miserable for yourself and everyone around you.

- You are envious of someone's talents, so you constantly put them down or try to undermine them in some way—and then hate yourself for it.
- You feel taken advantage of, so you act like a martyr all the time, instead of trying to talk out or correct the situation.
- You complain so much about your own troubles that you bore yourself and everyone around you.

If any of these sound familiar, you are experiencing a kind of personal suffering of your own making. You know better. You can do better. You can rise out of the condition you have put yourself in and fight with all of your intellect and will for the holy response to daily life. If you are in this predicament, God is allowing it only as a matter of free will. You are free to goof up, and that is what you are doing. Pray for the strength and the guidance to climb out of the hole you have put yourself in. Pray to know how Jesus would respond in this situation, and for the strength to be able to imitate His response. It won't always be easy, and you may have to swallow your pride. But you can do it, and God will help you if you ask.

There is, though, another kind of personal suffering that some of us experience, and it is the suffering that results from the weaknesses of our own temperaments. This kind of suffering is tougher to deal with, because we are struggling with inborn character traits that are not so easily overcome:

- You might be a melancholy person who is tearful to the point that you can't cope with the normal trials of everyday life and refuse to communicate with your loved ones.
- You may be insecure, and your insecurity could make you paranoid so that you sometimes imagine things that are simply not true.
- You could have a hot temper, which makes you quick to criticize and hurt others unnecessarily.

To a certain extent, this kind of suffering is something you must live with. It was given to you by God to develop a kind of humility. However, He does not want you to buckle under the weight of this cross but to grow holy with it. Don't put yourself down if there is something in your personality or in your temperament that causes you to blunder or hurt yourself or even hurt others sometimes. Pray for control. Pray for the grace to act like Jesus on all occasions, and work on this weakness with the same resolve you would a diet or a plan to quit smoking. This will be an everyday battle for you, a battle that you must wage only one day at a time. You may not win each battle, but you can win the war. Keep at it.

INTERIOR SUFFERING

Interior suffering is difficult to articulate, much less chat about with a friend over coffee. You can tell a friend that your arthritis is getting you down. You can go to a banker with your financial woes. But the moment you start talking about the pain in your soul, people get nervous. They'd rather talk about baseball or recipes or something safe. This is why you should only speak to a deeply spiritual priest or minister—or a spiritually gifted friend—about your interior suffering. The soul is too delicate for anything less than true counsel.

We speak of "spiritual dryness," those times when you find it difficult to pray. Generally, this kind of pain comes to people who love God very deeply. Sometimes they are beset with a condition that suddenly seems to deprive them of His Presence. It is an almost unbearable pain. People who suffer these interior trials turn to God—the only Person Who can help them—in prayer, but they find a complete inability to pray. They are gripped with a spiritual fatigue and emptiness.

Interior suffering is like falling deeply in love with Someone and then feeling as though you have lost that Friend. You feel you cannot talk to Him. Praying seems like a waste of time. The loss you carry around is like the grief we experience over the death of a loved one, and you are enveloped by absolute loneliness and isolation.

The reason God permits this is so you can fully realize that you must depend on Him for everything. Interior suffering perfects our love for God so that we can love God for Himself rather than for what He gives us. Saint John of the Cross called this dryness the "dark night of the soul." While this is a painful experience, it enables us to live with God in pure faith.

SUFFERING THAT COMES FROM NOWHERE

Finally, there is the suffering that seems to come from nowhere. For example, an inherited deterioration of the optical nerves causes an active young woman to go blind the summer before she enters college. A model father in the prime of his life discovers that he has terminal cancer; his family watches him slowly waste away. A flood rages through a peaceful canyon, leaving a family homeless with everything they had built over the years washed away in a single moment.

Anyone who has lived through a tragedy knows the feelings of despair and hopelessness that spring up unbidden. Suddenly God seems a million miles away, unconcerned with human life. Such feelings are not a sign of weak or crumbling faith. They are feelings that will come and go. In fact, God can use them to increase our trust and faith. It is necessary that we work against getting bogged down in feelings to the point where we see no purpose to our pain. It is when we find no rhyme or reason, when there seems to be no value, no point to a situation, that we lose sight of God.

God allowed this tragedy to happen. Can you accept that? Can you accept that He allowed it with full knowledge of the pain you'd bear? Can you accept, even knowing your pain, that He allowed it to happen out of love for you?

Don't be confused or upset if you can't answer "Yes." Wait and listen. The moments will come, among the aching beats of your heart, when the absence of anguish and sorrow will be your sign of God's Presence within you. As these lengthen, you should pray that God will help you to make them longer. In time and with prayer, you will feel Him filling up those moments. You can achieve peace again, perhaps a peace such as you've never known, by acceptance of His Will for you.

SUFFERING IS NOT FOR ITS OWN SAKE

As human beings we experience many kinds of suffering, and as Christians we realize that all suffering is permitted by God. We understand that suffering can help to mold and shape and purify our souls if we respond to it in the manner of Jesus. But we must not seek suffering for its own sake or wallow in it for no reason.

God does not want you to wave a white flag to life's trials or to surrender yourself to a false martyrdom. Only God chooses martyrs, and it is a sin of pride to believe He has chosen you. There is a very important distinction between true suffering and false martyrdom.

I remember an eleven-year-old child who called in to our show one night and told me she was having severe headaches. "My Mommy tells me to bear it and offer it up to Jesus. But my head hurts something awful, Mother Angelica. Doesn't Jesus want me to feel better?"

In all circumstances, God wants us to use our efforts to get well. Our first response to affliction should not be to lie down and die. Passage after passage in the Bible tells of the miraculous healings Jesus performed for the faithful and unfaithful alike. The Old Testament is filled with prescriptions for health and directives for controlling disease. The New Testament is a virtual handbook for spiritual and psychological well-being. God made bandages, ointments, and medicines just as surely as He created the oceans and the sky.

He does not want people to suffer needlessly.

My answer to the eleven-year-old child's question was:

Take aspirin. See your school nurse tomorrow. Ask your mother to help you get rid of those headaches. If suffering can't be avoided or alleviated, then it should be united joyfully to the Suffering of Jesus. But God always wants us to first use our reason and our intellect to try to get well.

- If you are an abused wife, He does not want you to sit back and accept beating after beating. He wants you to change the situation.
- If you are helpless and bedridden, He does not want you to dwell on your pain. He wants you to pray for others and be cheerful to those who are assisting you.
- If you are a lonely person, He does not want you to wallow in loneliness under the guise that it is "God's Will." He wants you to get out and do something to help others. To pray for them. To feed them. To talk to them. To stop feeling sorry for yourself.
- If you are a victim of disease or accident, He does not want you to give up on recovery or to become bitter. He wants you to fight for your health and to seek the best medical attention you can.

Suffering in itself doesn't make you holy, so don't go looking for it. But if you are confronted with a painful situation, your response can lead to holiness. Our attitude can lead us toward God or away from Him. If we suffer as false martyrs, we are being led away from God. But if we act with the resources that God gave us, we move toward Him. When all is said and done, if our suffering must be accepted, we can then accept it with the conviction of Jesus because we know God permitted it for our greater good. We no longer feel that we are victims of some cosmic circumstance or rotten luck. We can change our attitude of self-pity. We don't have to ask "Why me?" We can try to look for the action of God in every person, event, crisis, or celebration in our life.

UNITING YOUR WILL TO CHRIST

Catholics are always taught to "offer up" our sufferings to Jesus. So many of my Protestant friends ask, "What is all this 'offering up' business, anyway?" And a good number of my Catholic friends have heard the phrase so often that they've completely lost sight of its meaning. This is why I like to put it in a slightly different way. I like to encourage Christians to unite their suffering to the Suffering of Jesus.

None of this makes sense, of course, unless you truly believe that Jesus Christ came down from Heaven, was born of the Virgin Mary, suffered, died, and was resurrected for the salvation of all of us. But if you accept that, then it is only a matter of using Faith, Hope, and Love to accept your own suffering also. Once you accept this hard reality, you'll be ready to use your suffering as a means of growing in holiness and becoming more like Jesus every day.

God loves in a special way those who resemble His Son the most. Jesus was at His best from the Agony in the Garden until His Death. He showed us that we could weep and still have courage. He showed us that we could suffer and still be united to God's Will.

If you are caught in a situation in which you don't know what to do or where to turn, think to yourself: What would Jesus do? He is not some ancient hero who simply gave us a sense of ethics or a moral "to do" list. Jesus, Son of God, gave us a way of life, now and forever. In your suffering, you are uniquely blessed with a chance to imitate Him.

TWO WAYS TO GO

There is nothing that pleases Satan more than to see all of God's children confused and resentful about the suffering in their lives. Satan doesn't want you to gain grace and transformation from suffering; he wants you to rebel against God in defeat, to give up, and to throw away your potential for holiness.

But you've got a choice. With every bit of suffering that comes your way, you've got two ways to go. You can play into the hands of Satan and become hateful and bitter in your suffering—or you can grow holy and Christ-like. You know, we all understand the phrase "Nothing that is worthwhile comes easily." It makes sense to us when we're training for a marathon or toiling in our garden or raising our children or striving in our career. But when it comes to our soul, we figure that we'll take care of it when the time comes, as if we'll be able to make a deal with Saint Peter at Heaven's gate. Who are we fooling?

In my office I use a beautiful quartz rock as a bookend for the works of my favorite spiritual writers. I keep this rock there because it reminds me, every day, that Angelica needs a whole lot of purification. It's a cut rock. You've seen them before. On one side it is rough and gnarled, brown and ugly, the kind of common boulder you'd walk over or kick in a minute. On the other side, the inside, you can stare endlessly at ring after ring of pure, uninterrupted beauty, in every shade of gold and silver.

God knows you can be burned and broken and shaped and molded into a soul of extraordinary beauty. You will have to suffer with courage to get there. But if you put your hands in His, if you place your heart and soul at His Mercy, you will overcome whatever it is that you now face or will face, with a peace and serenity that will give endless meaning to your life.

The time to work on holiness is <u>now</u>. Sometimes life is rotten, and God permits it. In every case, from a broken arm to a broken heart, He is going to bring good out of it. But if you respond to this suffering with determination, bravery, and the love of Jesus, you can bring even greater good out of it.

Hang in there.
God loves you!

—4—

Why Won't God Answer My Prayers?

I'VE ALWAYS BEEN our in-house "Mr. Fix-it," which means that when the book trimmer goes kaput, I drop everything I'm doing and play mechanic. Well, it was one of those days. I had just fixed the blade that trims our Mini-Books when the collator went out, and when I finally fixed the collator, the motor went out. After a detailed inspection, I realized that what was needed was the dreaded Allen screw.

Now I am convinced that the person who invented the Allen screw didn't know what he was doing, because it's totally impossible to find a home for such a small piece of metal when you've got a wrench in one hand and a screw in the other and you're groping in the dark amid a greasy flywheel. That was precisely the predicament I faced. I was about to screw it in for the tenth time when one of the nuns came into the pressroom and said in a sweet voice, "Mother, you're wanted on the phone." The screw, the wrench, and my patience came crashing to the floor.

I was, shall we say, annoyed. I vaguely remember asking her what the caller wanted. After a few seconds, I left the room to answer the call. A woman wanted me to pray for her daughter's friend. She was brief, but all I could think of was how I would ever find that Allen screw again.

A month or so later, we had a problem at the monastery ($73 in your bank account is a problem). Things looked grim until one afternoon Sister David opened the mail and found a $1,000 check from a foundation. Everyone was ecstatic, but I was puzzled. I had never heard of the foundation. I pressed my memory. Nothing. The nuns had never heard of it. "This must be a mistake," I said to Sister David. "Perhaps they meant to send it to Our Lady of Sorrows Church and not Our Lady of the Angels Monastery." "Well, if they did, keep your mouth shut. We need the money," replied Sister David. But I still had to call the mystery donor.

"Uh, this is Mother Angelica, and I'd like to clear up the matter of the $1,000 check that we received at the monastery this morning in error," I said to the director, half-heartedly.

"But there's been no mistake," she replied. "Don't you remember me?"

I confessed I did not.

"I called you about six weeks ago," she said. "I asked you to pray for my daughter's boyfriend. He had fallen and hit his head on a rock and was in a coma."

Of course. It was the woman who had called me the day I lost my Allen screw. "Well, now that you mention it, I do remember you," I said, rather ashamed.

"I asked you to pray for Jerry's healing," she continued. "You remember that the doctors had said he had no chance of recovery?"

All that I remembered was that it had been a very bad day, and in my frustration I had said to the Lord, "Please get this kid out of dodo-land." Naturally, I did not want to offend this woman with the details of my short prayer, but I did ask about the outcome.

"That's just it," she said. "Jerry woke up at 2 p.m. that very day, ate, and is now back in school."

I share this story because it points up how mysterious prayer can be. Obviously, my prayer—however agitated—was one of many that were said for Jerry, which is an extraordinary testimony for the power of prayer. Prayer is the most powerful tool we wield as human beings. You can accomplish more with prayer than you could with a million men and women or a billion dollars. This should not be surprising. Prayer is the way we talk to God, the Creator of the universe and of all things. It only takes a small leap in logic to realize that if God hears our prayers, then speaking to Him is one of the most important things we can do in this life.

The problem is that so many of us are hung up on the fact that God is invisible, and since we can't see any ears, we figure He could never hear our prayers. We look at prayer as a one-man show, and when God doesn't respond to our monologue by giving us everything we ask for, exactly when we ask for it, we accuse Him of not listening or of not caring—or even of not existing.

In truth, we know that God exists. We know that He cares for us in a deep and very personal way. Scripture tells us that God knows how many hairs we have on our heads, and obviously our Creator Who knows even this listens to every word we say. Not only does He hear every word and every prayer, but He answers them all.

"Why doesn't God answer my prayers?" The answer is that He does. And to hear His answers, you need only a willing and humble heart.

SPEAKING FROM THE HEART

Before we start looking at God's answers, it might be worthwhile to examine some of our questions. How do we speak to the God of all Creation? Surely not as we do with pevery Tom, Dick, and Harry. But do we really know what we're doing when we pray?

Most of us don't.

There are many pitfalls people face in trying to pray to God. Some of us are simply tongue-tied. When it comes time to talk to God about the nitty-gritty issues of life, we don't know what to say. We miss the joy of speaking to the Lord about our own concerns and our unique love for Him. Many of us lean on the prayers we memorized as children. These prayers are beautiful, and they can lead us to great holiness. But we sometimes forget that plain conversation, like thanking God for your friends, or praising Him for the health of your children, is equally important. We fail to recognize that God longs to hear, in our own words, just what's on our minds.

Others among us pray in outbursts. These people come to God when they're madder than a hornet or when they are grappling with despair. Usually they cry out to Him simply because there is no one else to turn to. Their cries of desperation always pierce God's Heart, and He always answers with love. But God isn't just a 911 emergency number. He wants to hear from us all the time, not just when the chips are down.

Then there are those who are just plain shy. I have seen the most articulate business men and women turn pale when I ask them to say the blessing before a meal. They shuffle their feet and clear their throats nervously as if they were somehow going to say the wrong thing. This group just needs practice, and they need to know in their hearts that God loves them no matter what. The more they realize that it is God they're talking to, and not an audience or empty space, the more at ease they will be in their prayer life.

The truth is that most people miss the point when it comes to prayer.

- We think it is an empty ritual instead of a real communication with God.
- We only remember to pray in times of distress.
- We feel distant or unworthy, as if God doesn't have time for the little things that are important to us.
- We don't know what to say to Him.

Prayer isn't just a handful of eloquent phrases or holy verse. It isn't only a cry for help or a plea for forgiveness. Prayer is the lifting of our hearts and minds to God. For no matter what we're saying, we're asking, "Do You love me?" And no matter how He answers, He's saying, "Yes, I do."

BUT WHY PRAY AT ALL?

A freckle-faced little girl named Beth, who is eight years old, asked me why we pray to God for our needs. "If He knows everything, then He knows I need an *A* on my arithmetic test. Why should I bother to ask Him?" Well, God wants to hear from us just like anyone who loves us wants to hear from us. If push came to shove, most mothers and fathers could anticipate the bulk of their children's needs. But occasionally, they'd like their children to ask them. By the same token, a wife may know that her husband loves her, but from time to time it helps just to hear "I love you" out loud.

I'm reminded of a couple who came to me with a problem. Sheila was complaining that her husband was uncommunicative. They had been married for ten years and Jack seldom told her that he loved her. When I questioned him about it, Jack replied, "I married her, didn't I? Of course I love her. So why do I need to go around telling her all the time?"

What Jack needed to remember was that when you are in love with someone and want to sustain that love, you communicate with that person. At first, it's almost involuntary. You can't take your eyes off them. You think of them always. You want to be with them. After a sense of familiarity sets in, the love rises to a new level, carrying a new depth of knowledge and commitment. But this happens only if you continue to work at communication.

The love we experience with God is no different. For some of us there is a blissful period when we realize that loving God gives sense to the world and to our lives. Although we are light-years away from a truly spiritual existence, we have taken our first step and we're pretty enthusiastic about it. Gradually, we learn that knowing God and loving Him isn't always easy. Sometimes it's downright tough. And it is at this point that our prayer life either develops—and keeps us close to God—or falters, and leads us away from Him.

It's like any relationship, isn't it? A man and a woman fall in love, but there are elements of the unknown in each other. As they marry and make a home together, life becomes more complex, yet better, as everyday sacrifices cause their love to grow. But they must stay in touch with each other. They must work to avoid building walls between them. They must speak to each other even when they are weighed down by discouragement and frustration, or their love may start to wane. In this same way, you've got a relationship with God that you can ignore or nurture, reject or pursue. God's not going anywhere. But if you want to experience true Christian transformation, you must begin to pray and continue to pray.

MAKE GOD YOUR FIRST RESORT

Sad but true, many pray to God as a last resort, after all the doctors, psychologists, philosophers, or scientists have failed to give them an answer. You will remember in Saint Mark's Gospel the story of the father of the epileptic demoniac who first approached the Apostles to heal his child. When the Apostles were unable to heal him, he approached Jesus and said, "If you can do anything, have pity on us and help us." Jesus replied, " 'If you can?' Everything is possible to anyone who has faith." Quickly the father said, "I do have faith. Help the little faith I have!" (Mark 9:23–25).

That is one cry for help: the cry of last resort. In our desperate hours, when we are left with God and God alone—when no one else can possibly help us or save us—we always seem to ask God for help in a voice of unbelieving faith. But instead we should cry out with the plea of the leper who said to Our Lord in Saint Matthew's Gospel, "Sir, if you want to, you can cure me." He waited in humility for an answer. Jesus stretched out His Hand and said, "Of course I want to! Be cured!" (Matthew 8:2–3).

The difference between these two men is that one wondered if Jesus could, and the other wondered if Jesus would. The father of the demoniac was looking for a healing anywhere he could get it. He had already run through the Apostles, and Jesus was merely another possibility.

The leper, however, believed that the Son of God stood before him, and he knew Jesus could heal him. But his humility caused him only to ask Jesus if He would heal him. The man with little faith demanded a healing while the leper, who truly believed, humbly asked and waited.

The leper's attitude of humility is critical to our love of God, especially when we are engaged in acts of petition and prayer. Our humility must inform our hearts and our minds that we can trust in God's answers even if they are not what we wanted to hear. Our humility also accepts—even embraces—the reality of God's Power and Justice. It causes us to stay close to God, to speak with Him often, and, in every circumstance, come to Him first with all our wants and needs. This is why we should turn to God in every circumstance, every moment of the day.

THE HABIT OF PRAYER

God wants to hear from us, and He wants to be our first resort for all our needs. In theory, this is well and good. But unless we begin to make prayer a habit in our lives, the theory, like so many theories, will fall by the wayside of good intentions.

I have a few recommendations to make.

First of all, if you want to improve your relationship with God, you've got to take steps that will make you aware of His Presence throughout the day. The problem is not with Him; He knows you're there. The problem is with us; we're always forgetting that He's there. Aside from the question of manners, this puts a grave crimp in our spiritual journey, which is why I suggest that one begin his morning by dedicating the entire day to Our Lord.

There need not be any ribbon cuttings or fancy speeches. All you're doing is thanking God that you woke up. A short prayer that praises God, thanks Him for the new day, and dedicates the day to Him will warm His Heart: "Good morning, Lord. I praise Your Holy Name and offer you this day in love and thanksgiving." That's all there is to it.

Throughout the day you can pray to God constantly. Again, don't feel like you have to make it a big deal. Simply go to Him for help in quick, short petitions—for everything from health for a sick friend to courage in making a business decision. Slowly you will feel His constant Presence in your life, and you will come to understand your total dependence on Him. The power of these little prayers will astound you.

As your day moves along and the tensions build up, your holiness can be advanced by keeping God's Presence in mind constantly. Turn to Him. "Lord, help me to deal with this as You want me to." "Give me patience." Direct even the most humdrum events of your day to God.

The beauty of this kind of almost-constant prayer is that we become strengthened by God's Presence. Eventually we become transformed by God, by allowing Him to act on the little things in our lives. Instead of bulldozing through our day on a "gut" level, our first thought becomes, "What does God want me to do here?" In time, His Will becomes second nature to us.

DISCERNING HIS WILL

As our prayer life develops, we become more aware of God's loving Presence and of our dependence on Him. We speak to Him about big things and little things, about our dreams and our disappointments. We start to see God's Will actively at work in our lives.

Let's get back to our original question: "Why won't God

answer my prayers?'' All of us who have prayed for specific intervention or guidance from God have experienced the sensation of talking to a brick wall. We ask for a healing or for a new job or for peace of mind. But to our way of seeing it, we receive nothing. We still have a sick friend or the same old job or anxiety coming out of our ears. As far as we're concerned, God hasn't answered us. We wonder why He is silent.

This is where we must rein in our natural inclination to impatience and try to discern God's Will—His answer to our prayers—from the standpoint of a higher reality. We must try to see ourselves the way God sees us.

First, we must fully grasp that God does answer every prayer. But we must also know that He often answers ''No,'' that He sometimes answers ''Wait,'' and only if it is in accordance with His Will does He answer ''Yes.'' Given these three general kinds of responses, we must also understand that God's answering is often a process. His ''Yes'' could take years. His ''No'' could also take years and be interpreted as a ''Wait.'' There are lots of possibilities here, but suffice it to say that we can be sure none of God's answers will be pat.

So how do we know what He wants for us? How can we read what His answers are?

We can start in the present moment.

Discerning His Will is a matter of looking at our situation in the present moment and trying to see God's action. And it is not easy by any stretch of the imagination.

At EWTN we encounter this challenge almost daily, especially since we are almost always growing without the financial means to pull it off. After much prayer, we might discern that God wants us to take on monumental project X. We say, ''Okay, Lord,'' and proceed. The next day, we get hit by a dozen roadblocks and the whole thing looks impossible. We say, ''Help us, Lord,'' and He opens a few doors. We say, ''Thank you, Lord,'' but it turns out that they're dead ends. Two months later, the whole thing blows up in our faces and we see that the Lord was just trying to gain some time before we got engaged in the enterprise that ultimately reflected His Will, His true Will, which was monumental project Y or Z. But the detour we took toward project X actually prepared the groundwork for Y or Z, without our realizing it.

Remember, God acts in a completely free universe and He will not interfere with the free will He gave us. So regardless of God's intent at the moment, if all of EWTN's business dealings were being changed and frustrated by other people, He would still respect their right to choose, even against Him. I can't imagine how difficult it might be to arrange an answer to a prayer that involved a lot of people, all of whom have free will.

Now you know why you sometimes have to wait.

And sometimes you will get an outright "No." Again, it takes extraordinary trust to accept those much-feared "Nos." When we pray for the healing of a sick child and the child dies, we would much prefer to think that God never heard us than to think that He said "No." But if you prayed to Him, then He did hear you, and as tragic and painful as it might be, the truth—however incomprehensible—is that He allowed it because He knew He could bring a greater good from it.

Again, in moments like these, our spiritual companions Faith, Hope, and Love are crucial to growing in trust and peace of mind. We are so intellectually hamstrung because we can't see the world the way God sees it; we can't possibly know why things happen the way they do. We're like children to whom a loving parent must sometimes say "No." We must accept the fact that not everything we ask for is for our good, and that the only reason God might say "No" is because He wants to give us something different and better.

It is important that you patiently discern His Will in the present moment. You must always remember that God's answer does not hinge on what you say or how you say it or how deep your prayer life is.

God answers all prayers. No "ifs," "ands," or "buts" about it.

PRAYER IS NOT A SECRET LANGUAGE

There are no shortcuts to getting what you want from God. There is no special language or set of code words for getting the answer you desire.

I mention this because a lot of us think that there are some Scriptural guarantees that God will "come through" with whatever we want if we simply ask "in His Name." There are so many people who call the network in a fury because they've read Our Lord's proclamation, "Whatever you ask for in My Name I will do" (John 14:13). They've asked for healings, new jobs, Cadillacs, and the rest—all "in the Name of Jesus"—and when God hasn't "delivered," they get into a spiritual huff.

Asking in the Name of Jesus is not simply a matter of name-dropping. God doesn't have passwords or special handshakes or secret techniques for prayer. When Jesus says, "Whatever you ask for in My Name," He means whatever you ask for in absolute unity with the Father's Will. Saint John clarifies this in his first letter: "We are quite confident that if we ask Him for anything, and it is in accordance with His Will, He will hear us" (1 John 5:14).

If there are two perfect prayers in Scripture, they are the Lord's Prayer and the prayer of Jesus during His Agony in the Garden. For in both of these prayers requests are made of the Father, but always with the exception that the prayers be answered in accordance with God's Will. In the Lord's Prayer, of course, we say "Thy Will be done." And in Jesus' prayer in the Garden, He made His painful request: "Take this cup away from Me," and then added, "But let it be as You, not I, would have it" (Mark 14:36).

When you unite your will to the Will of God, then and only then are you praying "in His Name."

While we are on the subject of misconceptions, there is a dangerous and misleading idea that it takes large amounts of faith to get a positive answer from God. Again, getting the answer you want from God has only to do with God's Will for you at the moment. If God in His Wisdom determines that the best course of action or inaction is in accordance with your request, He will answer you positively. If there are obstacles to that outcome, He will work on them. If He deems that "No" is the appropriate answer—or that "Wait" is the appropriate answer—you will see that manifested in the present moment.

The fact that you have turned to God, even in desperation, shows at least a glimmer of faith. Jesus even said that faith the size of a mustard seed was enough. And we should never forget that Jesus healed the faithful and the unfaithful alike throughout His Life.

Faith is not a key that opens a magic door to overnight healing or instant riches. Faith is the belief that God has answered just as lovingly when He says "No" as when He says "Yes."

KNOWING WHAT TO ASK FOR

When we come to the Lord with a need, we can be perfectly honest. If it is a pain that we want Him to take away, even a minor one, we can unashamedly ask Him for relief. If someone is bugging us, we can ask God for the strength to respond to that person with patience. But the more we get to know God, the more we are able to understand how He works and what He wants for us in our lives. We learn that there are some realities that He wants us to face, not necessarily alone, as He is always with us, but on our own. We start to see the world through His Eyes, not just ours, and in time our prayers become more like conversations than petitions, for we have started to learn what to ask for.

I receive a lot of letters and calls from people who are victims of betrayal, especially the spouses of adulterers. A forty-five-year-old man made an appointment to see me one morning, and when he arrived at the monastery he was a mess. His clothes were crumpled, his eyes were red and swollen, and he was tearing shreds of tissue into little bits. I knew that a big hug was in order. When he spoke he dissolved into tears, and months and months of agony spilled from his eyes.

It was the same old story. His wife of twenty-three years had run off with another man. She was "in love." She still "cared about" him and the children, but she "had to live her own life." So many marriages suffer the indignity, trauma, and sorrow of adultery, but every time it happens it's a brand-new tragedy. In this case, the wife had been in and out of the household for five years, and had just a few weeks before asked the man for a divorce.

"Mother, I've been praying for a miracle for five years, just hoping God would change my wife's mind and that she'd come home again. Have I been praying for the wrong thing? Why won't God help me? What should I ask for?"

It is so difficult in a situation like this to see what is truly going on, and I certainly didn't want to register judgment on one side or another. But I could help this man to refine his prayers and to use his prayers as a means of facing reality and coming to terms with what was really going on in his heart.

Clearly, he was pinning all his hopes on a miracle, but so far his wife had chosen to remain unfaithful. He did not err in praying for the miracle, but he had to resign himself to the possibility that his wife would never return. I believe that God was showing him the hardness of her heart and preparing him to put his trust in God alone.

I asked him a few questions.

"What would happen if she never came home? Can you imagine surviving?"

"Yes, but it would be sheer misery."

"Would you feel worse than you do right at this moment?"

"I don't know. I guess not."

"Would you consider praying for the light to accept whatever happens—whether it's the miracle of your wife's return or starting a new life without her?"

"I suppose so."

"Are you to the point where you can pray for your children and pray that your bitterness over this situation will not influence or harm them?"

"No, Mother Angelica, I'm not to that point. And that's my real worry. You hit the nail on the head!"

Sometimes, prayer can help us get in touch with reality. As long as this man was praying for a miracle and only for a miracle, he didn't have to face up to what was really happening in his life. He was unable to confront his bitterness, and was powerless to do anything about it. Christians must be realists. They must be able to discern what is really happening in a situation and see the action of God in everything, even their heartache.

This kind of transformation in one's prayer life takes time, and is often very painful. Our prayer ceases to be a prayer of demand whereby we insist that God do things our way. Instead it becomes a prayer of resignation whereby we accept that God loves us more than we love ourselves, and that He wants only what is best for us. We arrive at a place where we can live with the answer we receive.

NEVER STOP ASKING

We are all members of the "now" generation, and if our prayers don't get an instant reply we tend to give up on God. This is a great failing of our human nature. Saint Monica was the steadfast mother of Saint Augustine, who was one of the most famous playboys of the fourth century before he became a saint. When her son was quite young, she went to her bishop to ask him what to say to Augustine. "How can I tell him that God is good? What can I say to him to make him change his ways?" The bishop wisely responded, "Speak more to God about your son than to your son about God." Saint Monica prayed for Augustine for thirty years before he converted. He was later named a Doctor of the Church and is one of the most important Christian writers in history.

There is such a thing as persevering prayer, and I want to mention it now so that you can get your head out of the "gimme" mentality with God. I'm not saying, "Don't ask Him for things." I'm simply saying that you might need to

ask and ask and ask, and that this might be His way of draw-
ing you closer to Him or of building your faith or of increas-
ing your holiness.

A woman from Louisiana called the live show one evening
when our guest was Sister Breige McKenna, who has a healing ministry. The woman had an eleven-year-old boy who
was paralyzed from the neck down. "For five years I have
prayed for his healing, Mother, and I've asked for the courage to stick with it. I've received more strength than I ever
knew was possible, and I know and believe in my heart that
my son is a perfect human being. But should I keep praying
for his recovery?"

Sister Breige answered with a story. She told the woman
about a family of seven from the Midwest. Their youngest
child was a little boy who had a brain tumor. In her beautiful
Irish accent, she explained, "The doctors had thrown up their
hands. 'No hope. No hope,' they said. But the family continued to pray for the boy's recovery.

"Every night before bed they would gather in Tommy's
room and pray for him together. Two years passed, and the
boy grew worse. 'God's made up His Mind,' the father said,
and he stopped praying completely. But the mother and the
children persevered. Slowly, Tommy started showing im-
provement. Day by day, he started to get better. And today,
he is as normal and healthy a child as you have ever seen.

"It was the father who told me this story," Sister Breige
continued. " 'If Tommy had been healed instantly,' he said,
'the other children would never have known about the power
of prayer and the need for sticking with it. And neither would
I.' "

God permitted this child's condition only because He knew
that this family—all seven of them—would be transformed by
it. So always keep praying for your needs no matter what.
Never, ever stop asking God for His intervention and His
Mercy.

Your relationship with God is unique. He has a mission
reserved for you that no other person can accomplish. Everything that happens to you is an opportunity to fulfill that mission, which you probably won't completely understand until

you get to Heaven. But to begin to understand your mission, it's important that you listen to God as He speaks to you each day.

Am I telling you to look for Him in a prophetic dream or a vision? No. So please don't spend your life waiting for a big mystical experience, because that isn't half as important as the way God speaks to you in everyday life. He's not going to appear in your living room and sit down and chit-chat with you, but you will encounter Him and His Will for you in little ways, in whispers and in other people and events. He speaks to you constantly, and it's a matter of practice to be able to hear what He is saying to you.

If you are praying for an illness to be healed, His answer is going to be pretty obvious. If it is healed immediately, His answer was "Yes." If it takes a turn for the worse, His answer for a physical healing may be "No." But what if everything just freezes, and the illness lingers and lingers in some halfway zone? What is God telling you then? We can be assured that although the person is not physically healed, there is a tremendous amount of spiritual and emotional healing going on in the individual. Additionally, this can also benefit the individual's loved ones, preparing them for whatever is God's Will in this situation.

We all have worries and concerns about ourselves and other people. When there is pain, especially another person's pain, we want a resolution immediately, and we see only one course of acceptable action. "Take the pain away." "Help me find a job." "Bring my wife back." "Heal my son's drug problem." But God is answering your prayer for this resolution in many ways, through many voices and even through His Silence. Listen to Him. His answer may not be the answer you want or expect right now, but He is telling you something at this very moment. Open your heart to Him and let Him in.

THE HAPPY STRUGGLE

It's a struggle, isn't it? You struggle to know what you want, and then you struggle with what you ask for, and finally you struggle with what you get.

We have said that prayer is lifting our hearts and minds to God. It is a love letter, a confession, the moment in our lives when we are privileged to be on our knees in sadness and humility, asking for God's help. Our acceptance of God's answers is one of the things that makes us Christian—tiny human souls in search of our God.

God hears you. He hears your cries at night, He knows how weary and tired you are, He feels the weight of your burden. He knows that when you are happy, you worry that your happiness will end. He knows that when you suffer, your aloneness is numbing. He knows what is in your heart.

That is why you must stay close to Him and speak with Him often. Once you realize that He is as real as the person sitting next to you, you can open your heart to this Divine Friend.

It's a struggle. But you are struggling with a Father Who understands your struggle, and with His Son, Who had the same struggle, and with the Holy Spirit, Who is going to give you what you truly need to persevere in the struggle.

God is on your side.
Speak to Him and listen for His answer.

Part II

LIFE AND LOVE

—5—

How Can I Overcome Lust?

T HE LETTER WAS handwritten in ballpoint on corporate stationery, which is why, I suppose, it caught my attention in the first place. It was from the chief executive officer of a Midwest conglomerate, a man who evidently did not want his secretary to see this particular piece of correspondence.

Dear Mother Angelica,

I don't really know you, but even if I did, the very fact that I am writing to you, a Franciscan nun, surprises me. I became aware of EWTN about six months ago when I bought a satellite dish. I have a home in the country and had purchased a dish so I could receive better reception.

Actually, that's only partly true. The reception I was most interested in was X- and R-rated movies. The first week my television was wired in, I came across you. A nun in an old-fashioned habit. I had not been to Mass in twenty years, and why I lingered for even a moment at your network is beyond me. Let it simply be said that you got my attention.

Since then, I've been a loyal viewer of your network, and I've never again been tempted to check out the porno movies. My life isn't perfect, but it's been better because EWTN helped me to return to the Church. It's kind of strange, isn't it? I bought that dish to look at pornography and I ended up watching a sixty-year-old nun. You're the best TV date I ever had. Is God always this sneaky?

Well, as you can imagine, cheers went up around the monastery when I read the letter aloud to the nuns, but they weren't cheers of surprise. Over the years, we've seen some of the strangest, sneakiest behavior imaginable by God. We get a lot of letters and calls from people who were looking for some "adult" movies and ended up watching EWTN. And at least a dozen times we've received calls from men ranting and raving for us to "get that nun off their television." We have to wonder why they don't simply change the channel.

To answer our friend's question, God is sneaky when it comes to helping people conquer their moral problems, because He knows that they just can't do it alone. You need God's Grace to overcome sexual temptations, and with His Grace you can wage a holy battle against your weaknesses. I want you to know that if you have a problem with this kind of temptation, you're not alone. Lust is one of the seven capital sins* that have brought thousands of people to our network in search of guidance. Sometimes they arrive "accidentally," like the man who was looking for some pornographic movies and ended up watching EWTN. But usually we hear from them because they've suffered the consequences of lust. Adultery. Abortion. Discontent in their marriages. Obsession. The list is a long one.

Now there are always some skeptics in the audience, and if you are wondering what a nun who looks like your grand-

---

*The other capital sins are pride, covetousness, anger, gluttony, envy, and sloth. Every kind of sin derives from one of these categories.

mother could have to say on the subject of lust, let me issue this warning: I have a lot to say because I have seen it ruin so many lives. If I sound "prudish" and "old-fashioned," well, so be it. But do me a favor and read this chapter to the end. Because if you are dealing with a weakness that has to do with lust, you have an enormous struggle ahead of you. The struggle requires you to use your intellect, to pray for God's Grace, and to live in the present moment.

"How do I overcome lust?" you ask me. You start by truly appreciating the gift of sexuality that God has given you.

THE GIFT

The reason I do not take the subject of lust lightly is because I do not take the sexual union of two human beings lightly. I believe that sexual union in the Sacrament of Marriage is one of the most eloquent and sacred expressions of Christian love.

When you are caught up in the throes of lust, you don't see sexual union as a gift from God. You don't find it beautiful or sacramental. It is, for you, simply a base emotion or a physical sensation, a sign of conquest or a Band-Aid for loneliness, and it is no more meaningful than any other animal hunger.

"But Mother, I'm just human," you say. "I have desires and sexual appetites. Am I supposed to pretend they're not there?" No, that is not my point. My point is that you are not "just human." When you say "just human" you really mean "just an animal." It is so popular these days to write off all of our weaknesses and infidelities to the fact that we are "only human." It's a convenient way to disavow our responsibility to ourselves, our neighbor, our world, and our God. "I watched an *X*-rated movie while my wife was out of town, but what do you want? I'm just human." "I went home with that beautiful blond last night, but what could I do? Everybody does it. Things are different today." "I picked up a skin magazine and looked at some photos. Hey, I'm human. What do you want?''

Well, if you are a Christian, what you want is better. And God demands better. God demands better because you are better. You are made in His Image. You bear His Spirit in your soul. You are not an animal. You have an intellect. You have free will. And, when it comes to your body, you have an extraordinary, wonderful gift of sexuality that God has given you, not to taint and abuse and degrade but to celebrate and glorify and cherish. And one of the ways you do so is by joining your spouse in the sacramental act of sexual union.

As human beings, we are wonderfully made. As David said in the Psalms (139:13–14):

> It was You Who created my inmost self,
> and put me together in my mother's womb;
> for all these mysteries I thank You:
> for the wonder of myself, for the wonder
> of Your works.

Our bodies are miracles in and of themselves, and they house the great gift of our hearts and minds. But that's not all. For Saint Paul tells us we are also ''temples of the Holy Spirit'' (1 Corinthians 6:19). And this is precisely why we are not ''animals.''

Those who enter the Sacrament of Marriage must vow to take the dignity of human sexuality very seriously. They must believe that when two people marry, it is more than the establishment of joint checking accounts or the creation of a household or the culmination of romantic love. When the love of two people is mutually pledged in marriage it is an expression of the Trinity, with the Father loving the Son and the Son loving the Father and the Spirit as the Love between them.

What has all this to do with lust? Well, when two people are united in their love and when they express that love in sexual union, it is, in every way, the perfect creative act. There is no gesture in the human domain that even comes close to an act of such perfection and beauty. The fruit of that gesture is both enhanced love and the bearing of children, and thus what always remains is something deeper and more beautiful than existed before. For Christians, this beauty is sacred. And that's why the problem with uncontrolled lust is not just an ethical difficulty or a mere matter of breaking some rules. It is a sacrilege.

Am I saying that sexual desire per se is a sacrilege? Not at all. Sexual desire for your spouse is part of an exalted creative act. But to indulge your sexual desire outside of the context of marriage is a sacrilege. It is a sin. And that's where lust can present some real spiritual problems.

PLEASURE WITHOUT RESPONSIBILITY

Believe me, it is not my goal in life to rap anybody's knuckles. I've got plenty to do without having to chase people around with a ruler. But if you are wrestling with a sexual temptation right now, there's a good chance that you feel confused and, on a certain level, uneasy. Admittedly, lust is not something that I wrestle with, but like all human beings, I wrestle with other temptations constantly. I know how it feels to want to throw in the towel and then regret it. I am not perfect, and in other ways I know exactly what you're up against.

If you are wrestling with a sexual temptation right now, your uneasiness is the Infinite in you that longs for something better. I suppose many people would describe your uneasiness as Victorian shame or embarrassment or some kind of repression, but from a spiritual standpoint I can tell you that it is simply your soul longing to stay united to the Will of God. This is why those who indulge their lust inevitably feel a sense of guilt or disgust.

Why are we surprised that:

- Lusting for someone outside your marriage leads you to feel discontented and trapped.

- Committing adultery leads you to feel guilty and lose your self-respect.
- Reading "adult" magazines leads you to boredom and numbness to the beauty of the gift of sexuality.

The problem with sexual indulgence is that once the initial moments of pleasure are over, an uneasiness can set in. You know you've done something wrong. Whether it's cheating on your spouse or watching X-rated films, there is a part of you that says, "Hey, buddy, you've just crossed into some pretty dangerous territory." At first you might feel discontented, guilty, and degraded. Eventually you are able to rationalize whatever it is you are doing. Once the sin has become a habit, a certain numbness sets in and you start slipping farther and farther away from any sense of right and wrong.

As the sense of right and wrong becomes distorted, sexual temptations become hard to shake off. Why? Because sexual pleasures always bring immediate gratifications, even if those gratifications are accompanied by guilt or remorse. This is why it is so terribly hard to overcome temptations to lust. But the difficulty shouldn't be the rationale for not trying. The allure shouldn't be the rationale for sin. As Christians we shouldn't be afraid to aim for holiness. We shouldn't be put off by sacrifice. We shouldn't hesitate to set our sights on a higher existence, no matter how many times we may fall.

The fact is that when you try to shake off the responsibility for your pleasure—whatever the pleasure may be—there is going to be a price to pay. People who think that you can have it both ways have bought the great lie. Somebody at some point is going to have to ante up for the so-called good times. Now there are some who would sit back and smugly say, "Well, they got what they deserved." But I don't subscribe to that attitude. I am worried about something far more important than your getting billed with an invoice for your transgressions. I am worried about your soul. I am worried about your sanctity. I am worried about the fact that sin affects not only you, but your neighbors, your world, and your God.

Look at popular thinking today:

- "What's the worst that could happen? If I get pregnant and he won't marry me, I'll just have an abortion." They are willing to sacrifice a human life for the pleasure of a love affair.
- "One night on the town won't hurt. If my wife finds out, she can divorce me." They are willing to profane the Sacrament of Marriage for sex with a stranger.
- "God made me a homosexual, so why not have affairs with other gay men?" They are willing to defy God's Plan just to get physical satisfaction.

If you carefully consider each of those statements, you will see a gross insensitivity to the reality of sin and to the fact that they are gambling with their eternal life. These thoughts are not the thoughts of mentally ill people. These are the thoughts of common, "everyday folks." This thinking process is so misguided, so self-centered, and so deluded that it boggles the mind. If you asked a philosopher to diagram the logic of this thinking, he would laugh. There is no spiritual intelligence at work here at all. It is the hapless excuse-making of self-indulgent people who are deluded by lies and are oblivious to the fact that they are destroying their own souls in the process.

WHAT YOU SEE STICKS WITH YOU

These times are no better or worse than the times of Sodom and Gomorrah, but they are different. I think one of the reasons I hear from so many men and women about problems that stem from lust is because in the past thirty years there has been a society-wide escalation in the amount of sex and violence that the average Joe (and Josephine) is exposed to.

We have become desensitized to it all. Now what do I mean by desensitized? After seeing all of this sex and violence, you'd think we'd become more sensitive to it all. But our souls don't work like that.

I'll give you an example. In 1939 when *Gone with the Wind* hit movie theaters, Americans were scandalized by Clark Gable's famous line, "Frankly, Scarlett, I don't give a damn." I remember my mother being surprised that we had strayed so far from the standards of decency, and I also remember thinking, "What's the big deal? I've heard much worse at my grandfather's saloon." Now I realize that my mother was right. It was a "big deal." Clark Gable's "damn" was not the end of it, but the beginning. You hear and read so many four-letter words in movies and on the radio and in books that your ears and eyes skip over them now. That's desensitization. There are so many nearly naked bodies on prime-time television that the viewer becomes dull to the reality that these are people, not just bodies, and that these people have voices and ideas and souls. That's desensitization.

The escalation of pornography, obscene language, different parts of bodies exposed, different degrees of sexual encounters portrayed or suggested—not to mention violence—is simply overwhelming. And the problem is that many people have become deaf and dumb to the transgressions that are encountered and displayed in books, movies, and newspapers and on television. "Shock" is not part of the American vocabulary anymore. When it's not a big deal to see adultery on television and in movies, we are accepting its possibility for our own marriages. When we laugh at "gay" humor, we find it easier to accept homosexual behavior. When we see prime-time families living together in sin, we perceive living in sin as an acceptable lifestyle.

We think that because all of this is make-believe that it has no consequences. "It's just television." "It's only a magazine." "It's just a stupid movie." This is where we really miss the boat. Sure, what you are seeing is not real, but the effect it has upon you is real. You think it's the problem of the actors and the actresses and the publishers and the producers, but you're not exactly an innocent bystander. You're part of the show. You're the weak, frail character who sits there blankly watching and reading all the rotted fruits of their labor. You're the one who is shoveling dirt into your own heart. You're the one who is feeding your weakness. You say it's all make-believe. It doesn't affect you. You're an adult. You can handle it. But Jesus says, "It is from within, from men's hearts, that evil intentions emerge: fornication, theft, murder, adultery, indecency, pride, and folly. All these evil things come from within and make a man unclean" (Mark 7:21–23). If you don't think this material takes its toll, you're kidding yourself.

The fruits of lust come at a cost. The cost is to you and your soul. There is no such thing as "harmless" sin. The moment you say "Yes" to it, it goes out of the realm of make-believe and into your life. It's your sin now. It's in your memory. It's real. It's not something you can shrug off anymore. This is why it's so important for people who have a weakness for lust to take a cold shower—intellectually—and wake up to the little con games and tricks they play on themselves in rationalizing the television shows and movies and magazines and books they tend to watch and read. You say it's no big deal. But it is a big deal, because it's a sin.

IT WON'T AFFECT ME

Quite often we receive calls or letters from men who have had an affair or women who are complaining about the lack of intimacy in their marriage. In an overwhelming number of instances, it was seemingly unimportant things that led to sexual transgressions and ultimately to the destruction of marriages.

A woman in her late thirties from New England was visiting her husband's parents in Birmingham recently, and they apparently had to drag her here to the network to be in the studio audience. I could tell she was unhappy to be with us; she kept looking at the floor, sighing loudly, and fidgeting in her chair.

As it happened, this young woman was in the middle of a life crisis, and she surprised me with a letter a week or so later. She told me that she was thinking about leaving her husband of fifteen years, and she wanted to know if she was doing the right thing. She wrote that she had four children, and was really torn between what was going on in her heart and what was going on in her head.

This sounded rather like many of the letters I receive, until she started to share details of her marriage, which she said was not going well at the time and had lost its excitement.

"He's not interested in me anymore, and our marriage no longer functions as a marriage. I know there is no other woman in his life; it's not that. It's just that he isn't interested in sex. I want a real husband, and for me that means a healthy sexual life. Am I wrong to push for a separation?"

I gulped when I read her letter, picked up the phone, and called her.

"When did you start worrying about your marriage?" I asked her.

"About eighteen months ago. I know it sounds silly, but I was reading a wonderful book about this couple who traveled throughout Europe every summer, and they did such fun and exciting things all the time; it really brought to light the fact that our marriage had become a marriage of strangers. We're happy and all. But we're not as close as we should be."

Strangers? Two people who were happily raising four children and had spent nearly half of their lives together? I restrained myself.

"Well, I just love this author. And now I've read all of her books. And this gal I know at the country club I suppose had something to do with it. She helped me to see that there was more to life than chauffeuring the kids around and making Frank's favorite casserole."

The friend. The author. These things sounded so insignificant, as if I weren't really getting the full story. But after an hour on the phone it became apparent that I was getting the full story. Under these two "minor" influences, this woman was about to turn her life upside down. She longed for romance. She wanted an exciting life like her newly divorced girlfriend. Everything in her whole life had been refocused on satisfaction, paperback romance style, and she was ready to pay the price for it.

I asked her to do two things. I asked her to stop reading the books she was reading and get out of her dream world. Specifically, I told her to knock this illusion out of her head. "You're being extremely selfish," I told her, "and if you think you're going to be happier walking away from a near-perfect marriage, you're crazy." I asked her to stop seeing her girlfriend at the country club and to start seeing Frank, her husband, as the gentle, loving, intelligent man she told me he was and had always been.

This is an unusual example, I'll admit, but if I had asked this woman a year before if she thought a handful of sexy romance books and a newly divorced friend could ruin her marriage, she would have laughed in my face. The problem is that it's easier to fall off the deep end than you think. There are going to be times in your life when you just can't handle such influences, but those are just the times that you're most likely to seek them out. This woman was at a point in her life when she was very vulnerable. She had failed to resolve the issue of intimacy in her marriage, and had let it fester to the point where some books and a conspiratorial new friend were enough to almost ruin her life.

I can't tell you what small incident could get to you, but I can tell you it's out there. When you subscribe to an "adult" magazine and tell me you can deal with it, I say you're fooling yourself. When you sit around and watch movies about casual sex from the videotape rental store and tell me they don't affect you, I say you're deceiving yourself. When you walk into a singles' bar and say you're just looking for some conversation, I tell you you've fallen for the lie.

Don't kid yourself. These small incidents aren't small at all. No one can deal with them. No one has ever been able to deal with them. You only build up a false sense of security. Your self-control just isn't that strong, and if you've got a weakness for lust, you're playing a mighty dangerous game.

TURNING YOUR BACK ON GOD

There are times when all the common sense and logic in the world can't compete with the overwhelming power of our senses and our emotions. I don't want to suggest for a minute that overcoming lust is easy, because it most certainly is not. If you are struggling with lustful thoughts or with a sexual weakness or perversion right now, you need more than common sense to pull you out of the situation you're in.

So I want to give you a very hard truth.

When you know you have a weakness for this kind of temptation, and many people—on some level—do, you can measure your spiritual growth against how you deal with that lust. The rules of the game are not the same for you as they would be for someone who has no inclination to lust. You've got to pray more, and it will be an ongoing battle for you to live a chaste life.

- When you resist the temptation to watch or read pornography, you build up your will and are better able to deal with the temptation the next time it comes along.
- When you avoid occasions of being intimate with your fiancé, you are protected from the temptation to have relations before marriage.
- When you stop seeing the person with whom you want to have an adulterous relationship, your relationship with God increases, and you are even further empowered to cast aside your feelings of lust.

It's a struggle to say "No" to these temptations. I will never forget the evening that a seminary student from the Southwest called the live show. Our studio audience, which was composed of a group who had traveled from Kentucky, was a little taken aback when the young man said, "Mother, I know I have a calling to be a priest. I really do. But every day I am hounded by the most terrible, lewd thoughts. It seems that no matter what I do, I just can't seem to shake them. What can I do to stop these thoughts?''

I explained to the young man that he was clearly being tested, but not in an unloving way. God was preparing him for a life of chastity, a life that for him would be a never-ending struggle and a beautiful sacrifice. God would not have allowed these influences to exist if He didn't know that good—this young man's holiness—could ultimately come from them.

This young man needed to understand that lustful thoughts do not become harmful until we become aware of what we are thinking, willfully encourage it, and willfully engage in it. This seminarian, in fighting his temptations, had not sinned. In his effort he even resembled Saint Francis of Assisi, the father of our Order, who actually rolled in thorns to thwart and destroy his passions.

The point is that you can ignore and resist temptations. As long as you are saying "No" to them, they aren't sins. It doesn't matter how many times you say "No." What matters is that you resist these temptations, walk away from them, and fight them privately and with determination, so that your will is strengthened and your soul is made holy.

The alternative is a terrifying one. For every time you weaken and say "Yes" to evil, you reject God. And when you reject God, you put yourself outside of His Light, His Mercy, and His Forgiveness. When you do this you live the lie, a lie that will work for you for a while, but which ultimately places you in a trap of loneliness and despair. If this is where you are right now, you know what I am talking about, and you must ask God for the courage to change.

It is devastating to realize that when you separate yourself from God, you wound Him. You turn your back on the One Who loves you more than anyone, Who has given you everything you have in this life, and Who has asked only that you love Him in return. If you can't think of yourself, or your soul, or your neighbor, or the world that you harm every time you mock the sacrifice of Jesus, then think of God, Who made you with love and hope, and do not disappoint Him.

OVERCOMING LUST IN THE PRESENT MOMENT

When you fight to overcome your weakness to lust, you are truly engaged in a battle. The battle is to save your own soul, and sometimes, when you're looking a temptation right in the eye and the promise of instant pleasure is at hand, the welfare of your soul becomes a vague intellectual notion. Your willpower collapses. How can you be vigilant? How can you maintain the strength and the courage to wage the battle at all, especially when your senses and emotions are beckoning you to indulge them?

You can focus on the present moment.

If you will take each circumstance, one at a time, and deal with it on a moment-to-moment basis, you can—with the Grace of God—overcome just about any temptation to lust. When you live in the "now" you can endure almost anything. The lust you have at this moment is manageable, because you are only saying "No" to it right now. You are reforming your life, moment by moment, taking each occasion as a new opportunity to say "Yes" to God.

When you live in the present moment, you will have both victories and defeats. But you've got to keep at it. In the present moment, the big picture—your holiness—becomes manifest in what is happening right now. Your progress rests on what you do at this instant. It is a series of tough, painful, wretched battles—but they can be won, with God's help.

One of the great saints, Saint Catherine of Siena, once fought a battle with lust for a week, and for her weakness to have been documented at a time when it was scandalous for women to admit such things, it must have been an overpowering temptation. One day, when she seemed to be tempted beyond her strength, she pleaded with the Lord to help her. The Lord appeared to her the morning after her trial, and she said to Him, "Where were You when my soul and mind were filled with these terrible thoughts?" The Lord paused. "Did you enjoy them?" He asked. "Why, no, of course not," she replied. "Did you fight against them?" He asked. "Why, yes, with all my strength," she said. "Dear daughter, can't you see? I was always with you. For the strength you found, you found in Me."

WHEN YOU'RE ALMOST OVER THE EDGE

I think God probably gets a lot of emergency "hotline" calls dealing with lust. "Lord, stop me, I'm tempted to drop into a bar tonight to find a woman." "God, give me strength. The guys want to throw a rowdy bachelor's party and I know I shouldn't go." "Father in Heaven, save me. He wants me to meet him after work, and the temptation is great."

These emergency "hotline" calls are the most powerful weapons you have against your own weaknesses and temptations. Use them. If you're in a situation where you face a temptation and you feel you can't deal with it alone, call on God. Begin to pray.

- You don't have to pray a long, formal prayer. A cry for help will be heard. But you do have to keep praying until the temptation leaves you.
- You don't have to run to a church. God is at your side. (There may be times, however, when your situation is so desperate that you have to go and sit before the Lord in your local church.)
- You don't have to state your case. God has witnessed the whole thing.

All you have to do is tell God that you need Him. That you don't want to offend Him. That with His help you can overcome any evil that comes your way.

With the Grace of God, you've got what it takes to be holy every moment of your life. You will never be faced with a temptation or any amount of suffering or pain that is beyond your will or your endurance. Saint Paul tells us, "You can trust God not to let you be tried beyond your strength, and with any trial He will give you a way out of it and the strength to bear it'' (1 Corinthians 10:13). But you must <u>allow</u> yourself to be strong.

You can walk away from whatever it is that is tempting you at this moment.

WHEN SOMEONE ELSE IS TEMPTED

I know some women who have a sore spot in their heart about other people's beauty, and they feel insecure if their husband happens to comment about a pretty woman. This is not what I am talking about when I say "lust." On the other hand, the man whose head is doing a 360-degree spin every time he walks into a restaurant or drives down the street is feeding an obsession, and he needs help.

It's hard to know what to do when someone you love is caught up in a perversion or a weakness for lust. If it is your husband or wife, you have to look at the quality of your marriage and make sure that you haven't somehow encouraged him or her to stray from your sacramental commitment. If you have not honored your role as a marriage partner, you may have contributed to the problem, and as difficult as it sounds, you must broach the subject with your spouse and resolve to seek counseling or work it out together on your own. A "holier-than-thou" approach misses the point. Try to help your spouse by removing as many occasions of unfaithfulness as you can. Help your spouse to be faithful by giving him or her a good home, affection, and shared joy. Sexual union in the context of marriage is a gift that has been given to you by God. The focus of that union is not confined to the physical, but to the wedding of body and mind, heart and soul. If you can affirm this love within your marriage, you will have helped your spouse to turn away from sin and be faithful.

Sometimes, though, things go too far, and people enter adulterous relationships or dangerous flirtations. The pain in these situations is extraordinary, and at this point, while counseling and discussion with your priest or minister or rabbi is suggested, prayer is your most powerful recourse.

Last year I received a crate of fruit from a young girl in Washington State. She wrote on the card, "Thanks for your show on temptation. Love, Kate." I guess the fact that she sent apples was sheer coincidence. Anyway, we later learned from Kate that her mother had had an affair with the family lawyer, who was an old friend. When her father found out, he walked out, and had been separated from the family for about a year. Kate was still living with her mother, though hating her behavior and taunting her every day for wrecking their family life. She wrote:

> *I used to scream at her at the top of my lungs every night. It was awful. I wasn't making it better; I was making it worse. My mother said she was "in love" and she pleaded constantly for understanding. There was nothing to understand. My father and I were hurt beyond description. I felt so lonely, I was suicidal.*
>
> *Then I saw your program on temptation and I realized that I was not exactly in a position to cast the first stone, for I had plenty of weaknesses of my own—including my desire to have sex with my boyfriend before we got married. Mainly I realized that I wasn't an angel.*
>
> *I stopped screaming at my mother and took your advice—I started praying for her and for Dad, too. This was about nine months ago. They're not back together yet, but Mom stopped seeing the lawyer, and it looks like Mom and Dad might start communicating if we're all patient. I know things will never be the same between them and it makes me sad, but somehow I feel stronger knowing firsthand what God can do. I'll never feel alone again.*

If someone you love is caught up in a lustful relationship, you must turn to God immediately and ask in prayer that He direct that person away from sin and back into a faithful existence. You must remember that, were it not for the Grace of God, it might be you out there in the throes of lust, and you must pray for the patience and courage to forgive the one who hurt you most. No matter what happens, no matter how hopeless or awful it seems right now, God will bring good out of your pain and the pain that has been inflicted upon others because of this weakness of lust.

HIS GRACE

It's got to be tough, being God, watching millions of human beings He loves make a mess of things over and over again. But in His great Mercy, He puts up with all of our sins because He knows we can repent and transcend them. Our ability to transcend them has nothing to do with how wonderful we are, but everything to do with how good He is.

If you had to fight against temptation without the Grace of God, you'd be a loser. So don't look into the mirror and say, "I don't need anyone but me." You need God for the very air you breathe, let alone the temptations you must overcome. And He wants you to come to Him first.

So if you've got a struggle, don't hesitate to talk to Him. If you have damaged your soul, you must make reparation to allow His Grace to enter you and heal you. Don't give in to your senses or your emotions or your feelings. Give in to God. Whatever it is, you can overcome it with God's help.

THE NEVER-ENDING BATTLE

You might be wondering why God allows us to go through all of this agony and indecision, why He would let His children battle with sin and evil and lust in the first place.

Wouldn't it be better if we lived in a world that was free of lust?

Well, as a practical matter, we don't. Adam and Eve, our original parents, have already taken care of that by desiring to know evil. They made a decision to say to God, "I will not serve." One of the punishments for Adam's sin was a weakness for evil, which has been passed down to all men. Facts are facts, and the fact is that we are all weak. So let's look at the world the way it is, not just the way we wish it could be, and see what we can make of it. Because if we do that, we begin to see that overcoming lust, as grim and difficult as it is, is an opportunity to prove your love for God.

It's true. Every time you are presented with an occasion of sin, you are also being given an occasion to choose holiness. They are simply flip sides of the same coin. Each event in life is an opportunity to choose God. If you envision the world from that standpoint, you lose some of the oppressive feelings you may have about sin and temptation.

The fight against lust can make you holy. Every time you resist sin, you bend your will closer and closer to the Will of God. You align yourself with His thinking, His strength, His sensibilities of time and place. You become less afraid of yourself and your weaknesses when you see the Power of God in your life and know that He is ready to rescue you.

It's not an easy process, this life of sorting out the good from the evil. We sometimes squirm because it seems so unfair. We go about our everyday business and then, bam, there's a temptation that is really tough to resist. We fall, pick ourselves up again, and fall again.

But these are battles that must be fought and won if we are to be God's children. This is the way it is and the way it always has been. My only caution for you is this: Don't kid yourself.

If you are dabbling with lust, don't pretend it's okay, because it's not. Don't walk into situations that you know mean trouble, because you're going to have a hard time getting out of them. Don't gloss over the hard truth that sin is sin.

Adultery is a sin.

Sexual union before marriage is a sin.

Indulging in lust is a sin.

Homosexual activity is a sin.

Watching "adult" movies is a sin.

Reading sex magazines is a sin.

Sin is not love. Sin is disobedience and pride. Sin is turning away from God. And the moment you come to terms with the Truth—the Truth that does not change—you have rounded the corner and are headed back into the Arms of God again.

You can overcome your temptations.
God will help you.

—6—

How Can I Free Myself from Guilt?

IF YOU'D HEARD his voice and had to guess, you'd say he was about thirty-five. Clean-cut. Well-educated. Probably from the Midwest. In fact, in lots of ways, just hearing his voice would have reminded you of a Norman Rockwell painting, he seemed so sure and friendly and sincere.

He was all of those things. At first. But as he talked before millions of our viewers, you knew you were listening to someone who had gone to hell and had come back to talk about it.

His name was Tom. He was traveling on business and was staying at a motel in Arizona one night when he turned on the television and happened across our live show. He had never phoned in to a "call-in" show before in his life. And for the first minute or so of his call, we thought he had just telephoned to say "Hi." He talked a little baseball and spoke about a few other odds and ends until finally the cameraman started encouraging me to help him get to the point.

"And what can we help you with, Tom?" I finally asked, wondering what had caused this likable young man to call.

More chatter. He continued to beat around the bush. The cameraman was signaling me to do something quickly, on the threat of cutting the poor guy off.

Now I've been accused of many things, but patience is not one of them. Ordinarily, I would have been pretty blunt, but the Lord was telling me to go easy on this young man, so I did. "Tom, would you like to ask us a question tonight?" I asked again, as gently as I could.

Then the dam broke, and it didn't take a minute to understand why Tom, at first, was hesitant to tell his story. As we soon learned, he had spent three years in the jungles of Vietnam, like so many of our troops. He had killed dozens of Vietnamese soldiers; that was war. But Tom had also looked deep into the eyes of a young Vietnamese as he fired at close range. And though more than a decade had passed, that face still haunted him.

"I've been to Confession," Tom said, "and I know theoretically that God forgives me, but God's Forgiveness seems so abstract and so far away. Frankly, I don't believe God could forgive such a horrible thing, and if He has, then I don't understand why. I feel so guilty that I can't see straight. And I'm so depressed—well, I even think about killing myself. I know it's a sin, but I can't help it."

By the time he was finished there wasn't a dry eye in the studio audience. And while some of the tears were no doubt for the reality of war, most of them were for Tom.

You see, Tom was not simply feeling guilt or the sorrow anyone would feel for taking a human life. Tom was not feeling guilt; he had become guilt. He was a living, breathing emotion, swirling in remorse, fantasy, and self-recrimination. To the outside world he was a responsible businessman. Punctual. Professional. Hardworking. But inside he was living a secret life of dark emotions, and his depressions and suicidal tendencies were taking over his soul.

But Tom knew all this. In his own words, he said he "couldn't see straight." He had clouded the issue so much that he felt not only a reasonable guilt for the lives he had taken, but a fabricated guilt as well.

Clearly, he needed the help of a counselor or psychologist,

and I advised him to seek professional help immediately. But his soul—as well as his mind—was suffering from delusions and misapprehensions. It was as if, for fifteen years, he had walked around with a wound that never healed but only festered and worsened, so that it bore no resemblance to the original wound at all. Tom had a wound that only God could heal.

When guilt becomes twisted, when it becomes an obsession, as it had in Tom's case, it is not God speaking to us. It is our own voice, and it is an abuse of our soul. For Tom was about to despair. He had forgotten what so many of us forget: that God is merciful, that He loves, and that He forgives. Tom had forgotten that God is greater than our guilt. Saint John assures us that even if our heart condemns us, God is greater than our heart. It is with this in mind that we should look at our guilt, convinced that God's Mercy is no mere theory, no pat answer, but is real and always ready to forgive.

I tried to explain to Tom that he was drowning in excessive guilt. While I did not know the details of the atrocities he had committed in Vietnam, I did know that by receiving the Sacrament of Reconciliation he had already received God's Forgiveness. Yet Tom's excessive guilt had shaken his trust in God. He couldn't grasp that God's Mercy was greater than his sins.

I can only imagine the memories of war that haunted him. He indicated that a day never passed without the scenes from Vietnam flashing through his mind. On a spiritual level I advised him to try to use these flashbacks for good. In the midst of each memory, he should ask the Father for forgiveness for all the atrocities going on now in the world. Whenever he felt overwhelmed, he needed to reflect on the Father's infinite Mercy on and Compassion for all mankind, which overflow when there is true repentance.

If you are wrapped in some kind of guilt right now, it might be God speaking to you through your conscience, which is a healthy, constructive guilt. Or it might be guilt of your own making, in which case it's probably keeping you up at night for all the wrong reasons. Guilt can be God's caution, God's sorrow in you for your sin, an understanding of your sin that leads you to great grace—or it can be a misunderstood, distorted, and misapplied emotion that leads you down the path of pride. Whatever guilt is, it is not just an unruly psychological response to something you've done wrong, to failure, to blowing a test, or to an inability to realize your life's dream.

It is much more than that.

GUILT AND YOUR SOUL

Now I realize that when I mention the word "soul," a lot of people start to tune out. The soul seems vague to us; we know we have one, but we really don't know how to talk about it. Most people can more easily discuss cholesterol levels or the stock market than the condition of their own souls.

What does this have to do with guilt? Well, if you want to get at your guilt, you've got to understand how your soul operates. And if you want to know how your soul operates, then you've got to know what your soul is. That is why I want to digress for a moment and discuss the "anatomy" of your soul.

You've probably heard that you were created in the Image and Likeness of God. But that's a difficult thing to imagine, especially when we consider that in the Old Testament God is described as a fire, a cloud, a voice, and a wind. Obviously, God looks different than we do—so how are we made in His Image and Likeness?

The answer is that there is one part of you that is made in His Image, and that part is your soul. When God created you, He breathed an immortal soul into your body in order that you would resemble the Trinity—Father, Son, and Holy Spirit.

This act elevated you above all of creation, for it gave you the opportunity to imitate the Father's Mercy and Compassion, Jesus' Humility, and the Spirit's Love.

This might seem complicated, but it's easier than it sounds. All you have to do is picture a circle, which represents your soul, and which is divided into three distinct parts. A pie with only three pieces. The three parts make the whole, and each part—or faculty—corresponds to a Person of the Trinity: Father, Son, and Holy Spirit.

- You have a Memory with an Imagination, which resembles the Father. In this faculty you possess the capacity for mercy and compassion.
- You have an Intellect, which resembles the Son. In this faculty you possess the capacity for faith and humility.
- You have a Will, which resembles the Holy Spirit. In this faculty you possess the capacity to love.

I know that this is a subject for endless discussion and probing, but given this simplified explanation of the soul, we will now see where your sense of guilt arises.

Guilt originates in the Memory and the Imagination. We commit a sin, remember it, and feel guilty about it. If we are experiencing proper guilt, then repentance brings us back to the Lord and gives us peace. We have guilt because we remember a sinful action, but our Intellect tells us that if we repent and ask for God's Mercy, we will be forgiven. Guilt thus serves a purpose, because it leads us back to God and to His Forgiveness. The problem occurs when you leave your Intellect out of the equation and your Memory and Imagination run wild. Your guilt takes on unreal proportions, and you begin to blame yourself for things that aren't even your fault. Unfortunately, this happens more often than it should, because we don't trust that God's Mercy is greater than our sin.

Bear with me and you will grasp a very important point.

Feelings are not evil. But they are not reliable, either.

When our Memory and Imagination are on overload, we lose sight of the issue at hand. It's like those televisions that used to have three dials, one for the color, one for the tint, and one for the hue. If you turned one dial all the way up, you got a distorted picture. This is precisely what happens when one of the three faculties of your soul gets out of balance.

You get a distorted picture.

Once a sin has been committed, your Memory is going to work overtime. You blew it. You lied to your spouse. You snubbed an old friend. You were impatient with your father. If you don't let your Intellect inform you that God is ready and able to forgive, you're going to be in big trouble. Your Memory will never let you forget your sin and your Imagination will probably exaggerate it. At this point, you don't have much chance of healing or forgiveness.

Now don't misunderstand me. If you blew it, you should feel pretty awful about it. But you should not twist and taint your soul by allowing your Memory and your Imagination, without benefit of your Intellect, to replay your sin over and over and to embellish it—and as a result, to become guilt itself. In your mind, you're unable to do anything right, and all your actions become faulty and inadequate. Soon you've convinced yourself that there's little reason to try to improve, since you're only going to blow it again.

Let me give you an example. I receive a lot of calls from people who have recently lost one or both of their parents. No matter what the age or the nature of the relationship, it seems that everyone carries a bit of guilt about the way they treated their parents. "I never told him I loved him." "I was angry and resentful in the last years." "She got on my nerves, so I was impatient with her." Everyone regrets the things they said and the things that were never said.

Some of these adult children are tormented by the fact that they put their parents in nursing homes, or that they didn't call enough, or that they never visited. Their Memory and Imagination bring back the time that they yelled at their mother, only now it wasn't just yelling, it was swearing at her. Everything gets distorted and they forget that they were not always ungrateful, but that they were loving children, too. Their Memory and Imagination will not free them to work out their guilt with God, to repent for whatever suffering they might have caused, and to allow God to render His Mercy. The whole thing becomes a gigantic waste, because the Memory and Imagination have completely taken over, and the Intellect is barred from influencing the Will.

If you step back and take a look at yourself, you'll see that you're getting nowhere fast.

Another example: working mothers. I am not one to encourage women to pursue careers just for the sake of it, especially when they have children who need them more than any manager or law firm or corporation could. But if you've got mouths to feed, you've got to work.

Should you feel guilty for leaving the children in daycare? Obviously, no one is going to give your children the love and leadership that you—and only you—can give. But you have no choice. If you let your Memory and Imagination get into all sorts of contortions so that you stew about it all day or night at work, then in those precious moments you do have with your children, you'll probably fret and frown and weep and be entirely worthless for them. But if you let your Intellect and your Understanding enter the picture, you will realize that this is just the way it's got to be. You can't do it all, but God can. You can ask God to direct you in your choices of day-care, and you can pray to Him to guide and protect your children so that they will know of your love—and His Love—even if you can't be there every minute.

Wallowing in guilt doesn't solve our problems or lead us to holiness. It is not God's Will that we become so strapped down with our guilt that we no longer accept His Love, the Love that forgives. When we become guilty we are not listening to Him, we are listening to ourselves. Our souls are out of kilter. We are paralyzed, frozen on our spiritual journey. The sorrow and the repentance that we should be experiencing are instead replaced by an overactive Imagination.

GUILTY UNTIL PROVEN INNOCENT

Understanding guilt is a very delicate business, because there is no handy rule book for figuring out what is good guilt and what is bad guilt. But you can be sure of this much—an

135

enlightened conscience, one that nudges you toward right action, is good guilt. It becomes bad guilt when it leads to remorse, despair, and self-hatred.

Our goal is for you to stop living at the Memory level, if that is what you are doing, and learn to use your other faculties properly. You need to understand your sin and to use your Will to emerge stronger and holier from a sinful experience.

A very successful executive I know was divorced from her husband. Sue had been a Catholic convert for about fifteen years, and it is hard for most of us to comprehend the agony and turmoil she lived through as she saw her marriage falling apart. Imagine committing your life to God—with a true heart and an open mind—and then making a decision to end your marriage. Sue lived in a state of raw pain, because her love for God was great and she did not have the ability to discern whether the ending of her marriage was due to a lack of will on her part or to the fact that it was not a marriage at all.

For three years she lived in guilt and confusion as she and her husband attempted to reconcile their differences. She became so frightened about the possibility of breaking her vows that she couldn't work. She took her pain out on her employees and started to drink heavily. At night she would brood with her bottle. She became a recluse. Finally, the marriage ended.

It is hard to imagine what kind of sorrow this woman bore. In this case, her sorrow—her guilt—was good and proper, although it was obviously not good that she'd taken out her anger on her employees or that she'd become a heavy drinker. But she knew that she had offended God, and this was good—guilt for any sinful action is correct. Her guilt came not just from her Memory but also from her Intellect, which told her she was breaking her Marriage Sacrament. She was not imagining anything. But she was filled with the horror of disappointing the God Whom she loved so dearly. She was living in a no-man's-land until she began to seek the guidance of the Church.

After the divorce went through, Sue visited her parish priest. "Father," she said, "sometimes I wake up in the morning and wonder how I can live through the day. I make it, somehow, with God's help. But my heart hurts so much I can literally feel the pain right here," she said, striking her breast. "My husband and I were so wrong together, and yet sometimes I wonder what's worse: how I feel right now, which is like a vile woman who gave up on her oath, or what we lived with for four years, which was a mockery of the Sacrament of Marriage."

"Sue," said the priest, "God forgives you. And He will somehow bring good from this. But you must forgive yourself."

As it happened, the Church ruled that the union between Sue and her husband was not a true marriage at all. Sue is now remarried with two children, and her present marriage is without doubt a true one. When Sue could finally allow God's Love to embrace her, she could see how God's Providence brought good out of much sorrow and pain.

This is a case of guilt about a mistake. We all make mistakes that cause us guilt, all the time. Most of them aren't as calamitous as Sue's first marriage. But nevertheless, they happen.

- We blurt out something to a friend that comes across as too sharp or mean, and cause that person hurt.
- We forget an anniversary or a birthday, and leave someone feeling unappreciated or neglected.
- We promise to meet our parents for dinner and cancel out at the last minute, making them feel disappointed and unimportant.

Why is it good to feel guilt in each of these cases? Because if we feel guilty, we are less likely to make our mistake again. Chances are, we're going to be more careful about what we say to our friends. We're going to remember our sister's birthday. We're going to make a more concerted effort to honor our commitments.

If we didn't feel guilty in these situations, we'd turn into rude, forgetful, reckless people. This kind of short-term guilt teaches us something, and we can progress in our spiritual life because of the lessons we've learned. This kind of guilt doesn't linger; we learn from it and move on. It is a healing guilt, because it allows us to examine our error, make amends, and get back to the business of pursuing holiness.

WHOM DO WE OFFEND?

Every time I hear popular psychologists trying to wash away guilt because it doesn't "feel" good, I get a little upset. The emphasis of so much of this "feel good" positive thinking is on me, the person, rather than on God, the Father, so that when life presents a difficulty we can only see it in terms of whether we can pull a smile out of the whole mess.

I'm the first one to say, "Hey, you matter. You count. Be strong. Be cheerful." It's just that I'm looking at your soul, not a bright "smiley" face. And if you think it's better to pretend that guilt doesn't exist than to deal with guilt honestly, then you're crazy.

Don't let anyone talk you out of feeling bad about committing a sin. If you feel sorry right now, I know you can be forgiven. On the other hand, if you've done something rotten and you don't feel a thing, your chances of forgiveness are rather slim. I don't want you to make a career out of your guilt, but I do want you to make intelligent use of it. You must allow God to turn your offense into something that can ultimately lead you forward on the path to holiness.

Guilt isn't a punishment, but a voice of sorrowful reason. "Joe, when you accepted too much change from that cashier, you were dishonest. It's all you can think about now. Was it worth the extra dollar?" Or, "Sarah, when you failed to be compassionate to that beggar, you were selfish. Now you can't shake him from your mind. Was it worth it?"

In these two cases, it's pretty obvious who was offended. The cashier and the beggar, right? Well, you're almost right. Someone else was hurt by your actions, too.

That Someone is God.

Our Lord tells us that "In so far as you did this to one of

the least of these brothers of Mine, you did it to Me'' (Matthew 25:40). If right and wrong depended only on the immediate people involved, we could justify a lot of bad behavior. We could cheat on our income taxes and say we weren't hurting anybody—''Who cares about the IRS, anyway?'' Or we could take cocaine and say that our habit didn't hurt anyone—''It's my body; what do you care?'' Or we could tease a senile person and say it was a harmless prank—''She couldn't hear me anyway.''

Applesauce! Every time you do something wrong, you offend and hurt God in addition to your neighbor. Your guilt is God saying, ''Look, buddy, you are messing up. You know it and I know it. And until you stop and repent, the world and I will carry the wound of your sin.'' This is why we must listen to God when He allows us to feel guilt for a wrongdoing or a sin of omission.

''But how could that be, Mother? Are you really telling me that every time I sin, God is hurt, truly hurt?'' That is exactly what I'm saying. And this is so important for you to understand. Your sinful actions do have consequences. They affect your soul. They affect your neighbor. They affect the world. And they offend God. God is the goodness in you that weeps when you err, and He is the joy in you that is filled with peace when you live His Will. God knows whatever it is that you are doing or have done or have failed to do. If you have sinned, you must go to Him and trust Him, because He is the Person you have failed. And He is the only One Who can completely forgive you.

A DROP OF MERCY

The idea of hurting God is awesome. It's hard not to get a little nervous thinking that your petty actions have an effect on the Creator of the universe. Most of the time, we protect ourselves from this truth by living a life of spiritual apathy. We go about our daily business without a care in the world, more concerned about our memos and our electric bills and our summer wardrobe than about our holiness. Thank God that you and I aren't God, because if it were up to us, we'd probably wash our hands of these selfish creatures called human beings. But our God is All-Loving. And He's just a thought away, ready to understand us, accept our repentance, and forgive us no matter what we've done.

I was in California a few years ago preparing to give a talk when I decided to take a walk to the ocean. I love the ocean. I am really amazed at what God did when He created it, and when I see His Power in the seemingly endless expanse of water and the rushing of the waves, I always like to play a game.

On this day I was, as usual, wearing my brown Franciscan habit, and as I passed by the bathers on the beach I could see that they didn't know what to make of me. As I strolled along, the young girls in their bikinis started pulling towels and blankets up to their chins, one by one, in a strange tide of modesty. When I got to a good stopping point, I did what I usually do: I stood about twenty or thirty feet from the waterline and called the waves to me. I figured they belong to my Heavenly Father, so I could call them if I wanted to. The sunbathers looked at me like I was crazy, but I didn't mind.

"Come on, you can do it!" I called. And I was so surprised when one wave heard me. Suddenly I realized that I was about to be doused by one of the biggest, most gigantic waves I had ever seen in my life.

I was so stunned, I couldn't move. Everybody on the beach was screaming, "Run, run!" but I could not move. My leg brace was firmly entrenched in the sand.

Suddenly, the wave crashed at my feet. My shoes were wet, my brace was wet, even the hem of my habit was wet. When I looked up, I noticed that a tiny droplet had hit the top of my hand. It was so beautiful. It glistened like a diamond in the sun.

The droplet affected me so deeply with its beauty that I felt unworthy of it, and to my own surprise, as I stood there, I threw it back into the ocean.

My odd little peace was broken when I felt the Lord say to me, "Angelica?"

I said, "Yes, Lord?"

"Did you see that drop?"

I said, "Yes, Lord."

"That drop is like all of your sins, your weaknesses, your frailties and your imperfections. And the ocean is like My Mercy. If you looked for that drop, could you find it?"

I said, "No, Lord."

"If you looked and looked, could you find it?"

I said, "No, Lord."

And then He said to me, ever so quietly, "So why do you keep looking?"

That episode at the ocean taught me a profound lesson. I think all of us fall victim to rehashing our sins and failings, reliving our guilt long after we've asked forgiveness. We fail to realize that once God has forgiven us, those sins are gone forever. Our sins disappear in the ocean of God's Mercy. We need not worry about them any longer—they are permanently enveloped in God's everlasting Mercy.

It is hard to work through our guilt, to be repentant, to seek the Sacrament of Reconciliation, and then to fully accept God's Forgiveness. Believe me, I know in my heart what you're going through and I know what it takes to stick with it. But you must remember that God's Mercy is just as broad and encompassing as His Love for you is deep and personal. He's looking at you—yes, you—right now, and His Arms are open wide. If you can give your guilt to God just as you give Him your sins, you will be healed.

HEALING AND GROWING

"Repent." God asks so little of us. And yet it's so hard to know what to do when we are swept up in our own smothering guilt. In the past ten years, I've counseled so many women who have aborted children, and when they come to me, distraught, anguished, and bereft, I can see that they are devastated by the realization that they have taken a human life—and they just don't know what to do about it.

I believe that the guilt over having aborted a child is one of the most severe pains a person can experience. I'm reminded of a letter I received from a woman in Michigan:

Mother, you won't remember this, but four years ago I called you to ask you to save my life. I had attempted suicide twice, and a friend suggested that I call you.

It only took you a couple of minutes to get to the root of my problem. I had aborted two children within six months of each other. When I told you, I knew you were as heartbroken as I was. Well, I know you probably won't recall our conversation, but you told me something odd. You told me I was not alone and that I still had two children, even though they had gone to the next life.

You told me to name my children. You told me to ask them to pray for me. I thought you were some kind of weirdo, but I had nothing to lose. I did what you said to do. Over time, I realized that my children were not lost, but were created and loved by God even though they are no longer in this world.

Two years later I married a wonderful man, and last month we had a little girl. We named her Mary Michael. This is a birth announcement, Mother. I know I love her with a depth I could never have had were it not for God's Forgiveness and healing Power. I've tried to warn other women about abortion, and I'll fight it now with an even greater love for God and the life you helped me find.

This woman had experienced an extraordinary healing from God through the Sacrament of Reconciliation. She had suffered tremendous guilt and remorse for her abortions and had asked God for his Help and Forgiveness. She had repented for her sins and was now healthy, fueled with a higher joy and understanding than most people today. She didn't sugarcoat her sins. With God's Grace, she had overcome her guilt.

WHAT I HAVE DONE

You hear a lot about "Catholic guilt," but I know from the calls and letters I get that we Catholics definitely don't have the market cornered. And I know that a lot of guilt is harbored in the hearts of homosexuals right now, who seem to be multiplying in numbers and in sorrow.

I disagree with those among us who fail to distinguish between the person, who is a creation of God, and the behavior, which is a function of the Will. The many homosexuals we've counseled have tremendous guilt, and it's the kind of guilt that is fueled only by the Memory and Imagination. This kind of guilt confuses the reality of a homosexual personality and character—the person—with the person's behavior, which is clearly sinful.

If you are a homosexual, you bear a unique cross. I can no more tell you why you bear this particular cross than why I must wear a leg brace and a back brace. Or why some people must battle with alcoholism. Or why Jesus, the Son of God Who came to live among us, had to suffer the indignities, humiliation, and pain that He did.

You should harbor no guilt for the cross you bear. You should not feel shame. You are a human being, made in the Image and Likeness of God. Your cross happens to be homosexuality. But you must realize that it is a cross. You must bear your cross as a cross, not as a lifestyle or as a justification for sin.

No matter how deep-seated your homosexuality may be, it is not a license to engage in homosexual activity. Homosexual behavior is a sin. It is not in God's Plan. You must pray for the immense courage you will need to be true to God and to bear your cross with acceptance and with resignation as Jesus did.

If you are a homosexual, I want you to know that I pray for you every day. I pray that you rise from the grip of your feelings and guilt, that you discern God's Presence in your life, and that your Will be continually strengthened to resist temptation.

There is no way on this earth that you can conquer your temptation to homosexual activity on your own. You just can't do it without God's help. That is why I believe so deeply that God has a very special love for you, because He knows that the only way you can find peace—the only way for you to have peace for all eternity—is to finally come to Him.

Take courage from the words of Saint Paul:

> Not that I have become perfect yet: I have not yet won, but I am still running, trying to capture the prize for which Christ Jesus captured me. I can assure you, my brothers, I am far from thinking that I have already won. All I can say is that I forget the past and I strain ahead for what is still to come; I am racing for the finish, for the prize to which God calls us upwards to receive in Christ Jesus (Philippians 3:12-14).

With God, you can triumph, and bear your cross with a dignity that will witness to the whole world.

WHAT I HAVE FAILED TO DO

At the network, we hear from people of all ages, all levels of education, all races, colors, and creeds. But for all the apparent differences, there are certain heartaches and grievances that no one seems to be spared. Most people call or write because of their inability to make God real in their lives; He just doesn't seem to be relevant to them. Then there are calls that come from the crises of everyday life: divorce, rebellious children, alcoholism, drug addiction, death, loneliness, adultery, and financial worries. Many people like to discuss theology with us. (For example, why do Catholics worship the Virgin Mary? The answer: We don't. We ask the Blessed Mother to pray for us.)

But one of the biggest problems I've seen over the past few years is a tendency among Christians—usually very devout Christians—to get all wrapped up in "perfectionism." A majority of these people are women, but we hear from a good number of men, too.

These people set themselves up to suffer enormous guilt simply because they're not perfect. As a result, they're "perfectly guilty"!

Many of them are the "superwomen" we read about in books and magazines. They take on family, career, church activities, charities, the works. They try to make homemade jellies with one hand and put a Band-Aid on their child's elbow with the other, all the while talking on the phone to a business associate. When they simply can't do it all, they feel guilty.

Others are the "supermen" we don't hear so much about but who exist everywhere. They get home from a hard day's work, eat dinner, toss a football around with the children, run off to a community gathering or a meeting, come home and talk to their wives, do some late night work from the office— and then wonder why they'd like to choke the next person who interrupts them. Again, they feel guilty.

Our mission in this life is not perfection, but holiness. God doesn't want you to feel guilty because you can't do it all. Perfectionism is, as a matter of fact, a form of pride, because you are not accepting yourself and your limitations. Some people get caught up in the "super" syndrome. Others start nit-picking at themselves over their own temperaments or personalities—and when they fail, as they often do, they are overcome by guilt and depression and sometimes despair. The only Person you have to worry about failing is God. If you fail Him, you should feel guilty. But if you fail some arbitrary standard of perfection, you should feel silly. You are running the wrong course.

THE RIGHT COURSE

If you trust in God and His Mercy, your guilt will just be a station on the way to holiness. You won't get stuck there, because you'll know that He's going to move you right along on your journey. You won't look back; you'll look ahead. You'll see what you can do now. You will witness to the Goodness and Glory of God.

Whenever guilt and discouragement start to get the best of me, I think about Matthew, the tax collector, and his first encounter with Jesus. Now you know that before his conversion, Matthew was no saint. He had his own theory of mathematics: ten for Caesar, twenty for Matthew . . . ten for Caesar, twenty for Matthew. So here was this petty, selfish man who was cheating the people twice over, merrily counting his coins in the little tax collection stall at the market, when along came Jesus.

Jesus simply said to Matthew, "Follow Me" (Matthew 9:9).

When Matthew noticed Him, Jesus looked him in the eye. At that moment, the tax collector was converted. The moment Jesus called him Matthew knew that he was unworthy, a sinner and nothing more. And this is why Our Lord sought him out; Jesus knew that he had so much simplicity of soul and so much love to give that he would recognize his sinfulness, instantly accept God's Forgiveness, and immediately follow the Lord to a life of great holiness.

What Matthew knew in an instant, it takes many of us a lifetime to learn, and that is that God's Mercy is greater than any of us can ever imagine. Matthew did not put himself outside of God's Mercy. He didn't pretend to be something other than what he was, a tax collector and a cheater to boot. He had the humility to repent and to accept forgiveness. And that is exactly what we should do with our guilt.

The soul is a wondrous thing. When it is in perfect balance, our Memory can recall all of our actions, good and evil, our Intellect can inform us of God's response to those actions, and our Will can execute a holy response. When we experience spiritually prescribed guilt, we are responding with remorse to the reality of the sin we have committed. But as Christians, we go one step farther. We repent with humility, ask for forgiveness, and know that God in His Infinite Mercy will wash it all away.

Your sins are like a drop in the ocean of God's Mercy. They are nothing unless you decide to cling to them and let them take over your life. Give those sins to God. If you are Catholic, go to Confession and receive the Sacrament of Reconciliation; you will be astonished at the grace and healing that will enter your soul.

- If you have hurt someone, go to that person and ask for forgiveness, and then ask God to heal you both.
- If you are punishing yourself for a past sin, ask God for forgiveness and for the strength and the wisdom to forgive yourself.
- If you are engaged in a sinful situation, pray to God for the strength to get out of it, and ask Him for His Mercy on your soul.

As John Henry Newman observed, to live is to change, and to enter the Kingdom of Heaven we must change often. Guilt precipitates change, the change that is our transformation to holiness. None of us can be spiritual pilgrims without throwing ourselves into the life that God gave us to live, and sometimes we sin. But knowing that we have sinned is a grace. Feeling guilt for our sins is God's gentle Hand opening our eyes, so that with our own free will we can find our way back to the path of holiness.

God forgives and forgets.
Throw your guilt in the ocean of His Mercy.

—7—

How Can I Forgive Someone Who Hurt Me So Much?

ONE AFTERNOON a young man came to our offices, asking to see me. Apparently he and his wife of three years were not getting along. Their life seemed to be one giant misunderstanding after another, and if something wasn't done soon they were headed for divorce court. He spent an hour or more with me, weaving his tale of woe, admitting that he spent too much time at the office and sometimes took his wife for granted.

Finally, I said, "Why don't you just tell your wife that you're sorry and bring her a dozen red roses? I'm sure she'll forgive you on the spot and everything will be fine."

"Roses!" he said. "Are you crazy? She'll think I'm stepping out on her."

"Look," I said, "I know women. I've talked to a lot of wives, and I'm telling you roses work almost every time."

"You may know women, Mother Angelica, but you don't

know my wife," he said. "I'll try it, but if I get in trouble you're going to bail me out."

A week or so passed, and I had forgotten the young man and the roses. A beautifully dressed young woman came to our offices. "I want to talk to Mother Angelica," she said.

It was the man's wife.

"I have a problem . . ." she began.

She then proceeded to unravel her story of woe, the perils she had living with her "philandering" husband and the lying and scheming she had to put up with day after day. "Why, the liar even tried to ply me with roses," she said indignantly. "I know he's got a woman on the side."

Oh brother, I thought to myself.

"Look, my dear," I said, "the other woman in his life is me, and I've been doing my best to get him to be the husband he's called to be. I was the one who told him to send you the blessed roses. Now I wish he had hit you over the head with them, because you can't accept an act of love without getting suspicious. I told your husband to ask you for forgiveness because he's been working too much and not paying enough attention to you. But now I see that you're the one who needs to ask forgiveness of him. If you want to save your marriage, you'd better run home right now and hope he's more patient than I am!"

For some people, forgiveness is the hardest thing in the world. They would rather give up a friendship or a marriage or their own salvation than to simply say "I'm sorry" or "I forgive you." We all know of rivalries that have never healed, of countries that have never sought truces, and of wounded people who refuse to meet their transgressors halfway. In a society that values power, control, and one-upmanship, this behavior is the norm. So much for brotherly love. The problem is that everyone is afraid of being "the chump." Heaven forbid that our neighbor should step on our toes and get away with it! We forget that there is justice in this world and the next. We shudder to think of ourselves as being victimized or taken advantage of or pitiable. Saying "I forgive you" is tantamount to saying, "You got the best of me," and we hate to admit that someone could reach into our hearts and hurt us.

If this attitude sounds oddly macho, you're getting the picture. And you don't have to be a man to get caught up in this kind of attitude. Christianity is not a macho religion. As Christians, we are called to have courage, the courage to honor God's extraordinary request that we forgive someone even in the midst of our pain. It is an awesome command.

If someone has hurt you very deeply, I know that you are experiencing a terrible torture of heart. This torture can be eased by forgiving the person who has hurt you. I have a hunch that you think forgiveness is something that it truly isn't: a feeling, an end to your pain, a burial of some kind. Forgiveness is none of those things. But what forgiveness will do is lift the torture out of your heart and embolden you with a new Christian dignity, the heights of which you may never have known before.

THE HURT

Christian dignity may sound intellectually appealing, but if you are suffering from a betrayal or a misunderstanding or a lie or some kind of deception right now, you may consider it a small consolation. It's not. The truth is that Christianity is the ultimate consolation, the consolation of God Himself, and if your wound is great, only He will be able to heal it.

For now, I want you to set your emotions aside—just put them anywhere, in an old sock drawer or someplace—so you will be able to understand what God has in mind for you. If you will focus on His Wisdom and the love of His Son, you will begin to see clearly again. Believe me, I know what you are going through because for years I had great difficulty dealing with pain and forgiveness, and there were times when I really doubted I'd make it. But God, I can promise you, will come through for you.

I realize now that in a strange way my mother taught me everything I know about love and forgiveness. There were many occasions of misunderstanding and hurt feelings between us. But every time we broke each other's heart, we allowed God to mend them. We relied on Him every day for our spiritual survival, to keep us together, speaking to each other and loving each other, and He never let us down. But don't think for a minute that it was easy. Ours was a love that was painful most of the time.

My mother was a holy woman, but she was not a happy woman. She easily accepted the love of Jesus, but could not so easily accept the love of her neighbors. Somehow, I fit into that second category. Throughout the years I tried as her daughter to convince her of my love, and I'd buy her gifts and write her little notes that I thought would please her.

But they never did. When I was twelve years old, I saved a dollar a week, every week, $52 in all, to buy her a beautiful brooch. I had the brooch on layaway, and every week I'd go and look at it, in happy anticipation of her birthday. Her birthday came, and with much ceremony I presented her with the brooch. She muttered something about my bad taste, and that was that.

I was devastated. For some reason, the brooch episode was more than I could bear. I rehearsed the incident over and over in my mind like a three-act play. I analyzed it, dissected it, pulled it apart and put it together again. I relived the emotions, the anger and the excruciating pain of her remark. Eventually, I started trying to second-guess her motives. Why was she so critical of my taste? Why had she chosen that day to be so cold to me? Had she always hated my taste? Was there something I had said or done to offend her?

My Memory had completely taken over and my attitude toward buying gifts for others was permanently altered. You and I have talked before about the Memory and the Intellect and the Will, the three parts of the soul that correspond to the Father and the Son and the Holy Spirit. When you are hurt, your Memory and Imagination can flood your soul with pain, replaying situations and confrontations, making you wish you had said or done this or that. This fruitless assault buries the Intellect and the Will in the dust of your passion. You can become obsessed with a painful event, and you can lose sight of the Christian response to your situation.

When my mother criticized the brooch I gave her, my Intellect took a vacation and my Memory started churning out distortions. I was like an eight-millimeter projector that was frozen on a certain frame and the rest of the show, my life, was just flapping and sputtering in the air. Saint Paul says we should forgive before sundown—"Never let the sun set on your anger or else you will give the devil a foothold" (Ephesians 4:26–27). But I held on to my pain for a few weeks. That was how long it took me to get over my hurt. I could understand that my mother meant me no harm. It had not even dawned on her that her lack of gratitude for my gift had caused me pain. But at the time I had no idea what forgiveness was, or what to expect from it. And I think a lot of people are in the same boat.

FORGIVENESS IS NOT A FEELING

Forgiveness isn't a one-minute panacea or a way to "feel better fast." You won't find it in a cure-all book for positive thinkers or a training film for people who want to get ahead in the world. It won't make the initial pain go away. So if you are hurt, don't expect the anguish you feel to disappear like a rabbit in thin air the moment you say "I forgive you."

Forgiveness is not always a feeling.

I know a lot of people think that when they say the magic words "I forgive you" that all will be forgotten, as if forgiveness brings on some kind of blissful spiritual amnesia. I'm afraid that's not the case. There are some things in this life that you will never forget. An accountant we know told us that he was sitting casually at his breakfast table one morning reading the newspaper, as he has done every day of his life, when an angry fist broke through the sports section and popped him right in the nose. He was miffed about losing the box scores, but more than that, he was flabbergasted. The fist belonged to his gentle wife. "What on earth was that for?" he asked incredulously. "I just remembered something you did twenty years ago," she snapped back. There isn't any one of us who can't go back years ago and remember something that hurt us. This doesn't mean that the offense wasn't forgiven; it only means that the memory can remain. We just need to be sure that we don't brood on or reenact the scene when it comes to mind down the road.

Other people think that forgiveness isn't "real" if you aren't all smiles and hugs and kisses when you offer it. This is a great misconception, and it stops a lot of people from being true Christians. If someone has wronged you, you are not required to think they're wonderful for doing it. You can despise what they did to you, and tell them so. You can tell them it was lousy and that you feel lousy and that you forgive them in spite of all that. The Lord asked us to forgive, but He never asked us to feel like forgiving. You must decide to forgive just like you decide to love. None of this has to come naturally, and if you are expecting to develop the natural inclination to forgive, you're going to wait a long time.

As Christians, we don't forgive someone because it makes us feel like a nice person or because it's sweet, but because it's hard. The very difficulty we have in summoning true forgiveness out of our hearts makes us resemble Jesus.

Forgiveness is the first step on the long road to healing. It allows both the offender and the wounded to recover spiritually from the wrong that has been committed. At the end of the road, the offender is able to repent and the wounded person is able to imitate Jesus.

Forgiveness is not a shortcut to happiness, but the long haul to joy.

If you have pain in your heart, you can decide today to be healed by the power of God's Grace through forgiveness. You're probably always going to wonder why you were hurt, but you're not going to worry about it anymore. And in the end, as remarkable as it sounds, you're going to thank God for giving you the opportunity to resemble His Son.

THE ROAD TO FORGIVENESS

When we first started accepting "call-ins" on EWTN, our audience became aware of something we had known for a long time: that there is an extraordinary amount of pain in this world. There is something sobering and affecting about listening to the trials of your fellow human beings, and as we try to discern the holiness and good in all of our actions, we learn how to see God in all things, joyful and sorrowful. Sometimes it is overwhelming. Just when we think we have heard the most heartbreaking story ever told, the phone rings again or the mail comes in or there is a knock at the door, and someone tells us a story of even greater agony. The nuns do have their lighter moments, but they spend much of their time in prayer, asking God to heal the broken hearts and wounded spirits who need His Grace, and to forgive those who have so blindly wounded Him and His children.

Your wound may be fresh and your pain and outrage may be completely justified.

- You might be a parent who spent years of sacrifice raising your child, only to have him or her run away or rebel in devastating ways like drugs or sex or alcohol abuse.
- You might be a spouse who served your marriage with a glad and open heart, only to have your husband or wife run off with another person.
- You might be a business partner who trusted your associate, only to discover he or she has been embezzling from the company.
- You might have confided something important to a very good friend, only to find he or she has violated your confidence.
- You might be a young woman who has found herself pregnant, only to discover that your boyfriend "doesn't love you" anymore.

What do you do when your pain is so justified? How do you respond when it feels so righteous to stew in your anger and resentment and contempt?

You try to think and act like Jesus. If, for example, you have recently been hurt by someone, you should resist your natural inclination to share your tragedy with all your friends and relatives, the people who are "on your side." Jesus confided secretly in His Father, and His is a great lesson for us all. Spreading the pain does nothing to alleviate it, and if the truth be known, you most often are simply boring people or making their lives miserable. Worse, our tendency at these times is to cry on the shoulders of those people who will give us dangerous sympathy and short-term advice, the kind of counsel that leads us away from reconciliation and toward outrage and resentment and bitterness.

I am not saying you should keep everything inside you, but that you should exercise caution in whom you turn to in moments of human pain. Seek guidance from people whose wisdom and prudence will help you form a response that will truly heal you and your oppressor in the long run. It might be a priest or a minister or a rabbi, or a good friend who can lend a spiritual ear.

The point is that you are in a dangerous position now. You have been truly wronged and your indignation could arm you with a curled lip and the desire for revenge. The truth of your injustice makes you feel secure in your hatred. People will lead you down the path of resentment, cheering you on to your own destruction. Suddenly you will be locked into the position of "getting even." Make no mistake: no one means you harm. In fact, everyone thinks that they are building you back up again. But what really happens is that you lose the ability to discern right from wrong, and you avoid the difficult but necessary Christian response. The result is that whatever your initial wound was, it is far worse now because now you have succumbed to the temptation to hate.

In the meantime, another danger in trying to rally support from friends after you've been hurt by someone is the likelihood that the very person who hurt you will eventually hear about the problem from one of your friends. Sometimes this happens because your friends are trying to help the situation, but all they do is add to the problem.

Suppose you and I had a disagreement. We each tell two or three people, and they in turn tell two or three other people, like the child's game of "Telephone." By the time it gets back to you and me, it will probably be blown out of all proportion to the actual disagreement.

The problem is not your momentary anger but the long, seething resentment and bitterness that you feel. A friend hurts you, so you cast aside the friendship and never find out what really happened. Your child says something in anger, and you give her the silent treatment for days. Your husband is lazy around the house, and instead of asking him to help you, you stomp about in a constant rage.

When you're on the road to forgiveness, you circumvent all of these self-destructive feelings and vengeful behavior and replace them with an objective, determined effort to love. You protect your heart from hardening to all feelings and stop yourself from becoming a callous, cynical human being. Your path is the path of Jesus instead of the course of your own emotions. And once you arrive at a true state of forgiveness, your heart becomes open to compassion and understanding.

WE FORGIVE BECAUSE WE HAVE BEEN FORGIVEN

Some of your pain will never go away. It will become your hidden cross, known to you and God alone.

This is the cross of Jesus. As Christians, we bear our crosses because we love God and we long to live in the holiness and light of His Son. We are not gluttons for punishment. Our lives are not some kind of spiritual endurance test designed to see how much punishment and humiliation we can take from the world until we collapse in despair. But we do accept the responsibility to radiate the love of Jesus to the world. And part of that responsibility calls us to accept whatever it is that comes our way with a loving detachment.

We forgive others because God forgives us. It is so hard for us to grasp the true meaning of His Forgiveness. We hear Jesus' words "Father, forgive them; they do not know what they are doing" (Luke 23:34), and we are flooded with the Mercy of this God Who asked His Father to forgive—not just pardon or excuse or overlook—but fully forgive the sins of His children. Sometimes I shake my head in quiet wonder, thinking about the love of the Son of God Who, nailed to a crude wooden cross, His Body bleeding in excruciating pain, lifted His Head and asked that the foolish, cruel, ignorant people below, the people who would not listen to Him and who did not believe in Him, would still be forgiven.

Jesus' act of forgiveness did not take away His pain, and your forgiveness will not take away yours. But Jesus' forgiveness manifested the purity of His Soul before the Father, and He merited forgiveness for the many who were looking up at Him, for the thief on the cross, for the centurion below, and for people of all time.

You and I may never fully understand in this life why God permitted His Son to suffer such brutality and humiliation. Neither will we fully understand why most of the injustices we suffer in our own lives have been permitted by God. When people ask me tough questions like, "Why was my six-year-old son murdered? What possible good could come from that?" or "How could God have allowed my husband to molest my child?" I have to tell them I do not know. I cannot promise them that they will ever, in this life, understand why. But I can tell them with certainty that they will, in the next life, as preposterous and incomprehensible as it sounds, thank God for bringing good out of whatever caused them to suffer here in this life. They will thank God for the opportunity of forgiving one another and of growing in the likeness of His Son.

DO NOT JUDGE

When I am in a situation where it is going to be really hard to forgive someone, I ask God to help me realize that no matter what anyone has done to us, our God has forgiven us for much more. So if you are in some kind of agony and it looks like you can't muster up the courage to forgive just yet, ask God to help you recall the depth and breadth of the mercy He personally has bestowed upon you.

This is not exactly a household hint. When someone has insulted us, made a fool of us, or taken advantage of us, it is not standard behavior to smile a generous smile and think, "Oh well, I've done much worse in my day and God has always forgiven me. I'll just reach out and tell that person that he's forgiven, and to sin no more." On the contrary: we are burning with rage or shame or distress. We'd like to throw eggs at his door or clobber him good with a two-by-four. These are the moments to recall the precise wording of the Lord's Prayer: "And forgive us our trespasses, as we forgive those who trespass against us."

"As we forgive those who trespass against us." A deal is a deal. When we forgive others, we must enlist an attitude of compassion. Jesus tells us: "Be compassionate as your Father is compassionate. Do not judge, and you will not be judged yourselves; do not condemn, and you will not be condemned yourselves" (Luke 6:36–37). When we keep before us the reality of our own sins, we are not so quick to hate those who sin against us.

Compassion arises most often from having "been there." A woman who has gone through the agony of divorce is not so quick to judge a terrible marriage. A man who has lost his business does not look down upon someone who is having financial woes. If you have experienced a trial of some kind, it prepares you to understand the sins and failures of others. But none of us has been through it all. And when we forgive others, we must offer compassion whether we have "been there" or not. When we are humble enough to realize that it is God's Grace, not our own prowess or discipline or innate goodness, that has prevented us from doing far worse than the tremendous evil that we've already done, we can open our hearts to those who need it most.

Some of our cameramen and production people went to New York City last year to interview Mother Clara Hale, a saintly woman who cares for the infants of drug-addicted mothers. A couple of the crew members were touring Manhattan for the first time. When they saw Times Square, they were appalled. "You wouldn't believe it. They were selling drugs on the sidewalk and trading sex and money just like baseball cards," they said. "You would have hated it, Mother." I'm sure I would have been heartbroken and disgusted. But the fact remains that it is inadequate for a Christian to simply be disgusted or horrified at sin. We bear the burden of separating the sin from the sinner, and loving the sinner no matter what. I can't relate to the despair that drives people to destroy themselves with drugs, let alone to sell their bodies and souls in Times Square. But that doesn't mean I am not to have compassion for these young people, or that I am not to ask, as Jesus has, that they be forgiven and led to God.

I can't imagine what it must have been like for Jesus, Who after teaching and loving the impetuous Peter, after being so close to him, was denied three times. Can you calculate the pain of a spouse or a friend saying about you, "Never heard of the guy" or "No pal of mine" or "Sorry, wrong number." Can you picture forgiving a person like that?

Is this a challenge? You better believe it. And before you start to say that all of this Christianity "stuff" is too hard, let me give you some good news. You don't have to do this alone. You don't have to be a superman or a superwoman to forgive the unforgivable, because God already has. And He will help you to forgive the worst of sins committed against you and against the world, if you simply ask Him for His help. For example, pray:

Oh God, help me to forgive. I want to be like You but I find it difficult. Bless the ones who offended me and give them grace to see themselves. I give you this pain

*in union with the pain of Jesus on the Cross. "Father,
forgive them; they do not know what they are doing."*

DON'T BE FOOLISH

It is spiritually emboldening to bear the pain of a true injustice, but it's downright silly to suffer pain over incidents
and words that are simply misunderstandings. We've all done
it. Someone doesn't write you a letter for several months and
you think they hate you. Your husband comes home late one
night and you think he's running around. Appearances are
troublesome beasts. It doesn't make sense to get caught up in
the process of forgiving someone for something they haven't
even done.

I mention this because there's something in our nature that
causes many people to suffer for absolutely no reason. I recall
one woman who was simply riddled with agony. She told me
that a neighbor whom she had helped and counseled and
nursed during an illness was no longer speaking to her.

"I was downtown, Mother, and this woman was walking
on my side of the street, saw me, and crossed the street and
went in another direction. After all I had done for her. I had
given her hours of care and, if I may say so, not a little bit
of money. It's as plain as day that she was taking me for a
ride. How am I supposed to forgive her?"

"Have you talked to this woman about her odd behavior?"
I asked, wondering what could have turned this friendship
upside down.

"Well, no," the woman responded. "What would I have
said to her? Thanks for making a fool of me?"

I didn't believe my ears. But then this is the way we are.
I told my visitor to call her friend right then and there, in my
office, and she did it with the reluctance of a young child. As
it turned out, her friend had just been to the dentist's office,
had a mouthful of novocaine, and was so embarrassed she
had not wanted anyone to see her. Why had she crossed the
street? To get to the other side, of course! It was indeed a

joke, but not a very funny one because my visitor had spent weeks wondering how to forgive this woman for an imagined offense.

Life is too short, my friend. Whatever it is you are mulling over in your heart, whatever pain it is that has gripped your memory, check it out. Pick up the phone. Write a letter if you feel more comfortable or if you are too shy to confront it directly; whatever way you choose is okay. But make sure you know what is really going on. Jesus does not want you to bear a self-imposed cross. Your own cross is heavy enough without your adding misunderstandings and self-inflicted wounds to it.

DOES IT MATTER?

Our goal as Christians is to develop a forgiving nature. Our goal is to bear our own cross with dignity and love. Our goal is to build a sense of loving detachment from this world.

Our goal is not to get bent out of shape about nickel-and-dime transgressions like dirty socks and messy toothpaste tubes. In the process of counseling people on forgiveness, I have encountered many instances where it would have been a little bit easier just to overlook the offense. "She never returned my yellow dress." "He owes me $20 and won't pay it back." "They always cheat at bridge." I am not suggesting for a minute that we avoid an opportunity to be holy or to forgive, but I am calling for a little discretion as to what bugs us.

Maybe it's the Italian in me, but if your husband's been throwing the wet towels on the floor for twenty years, what good is your forgiveness? I mean, why bother? But it's not just married couples—I've seen it here at the monastery as well. When you live with fifteen women, some of them for more than thirty years, you can start to develop a few pet peeves. If I put my mind to it, I could spend many a waking hour forgiving my nuns and my staff for all of their little ways and habits and mistakes. And if they were to focus solely on

Angelica, they could spend the full twenty-four hours a day trying to forgive me of my transgressions. To what end?

I know that practice makes perfect, but if we were a little bit more selective about what bothers us we might have more spiritual energy to devote to the "biggies." Concentrating on the little things too much indicates a kind of self-centeredness, an emphasis on "How does this affect me?" rather than "Does it really matter?" Sometimes it is better to simply accept certain temperamental qualities and personality traits in those we love (and those we are trying to love) and just get on with our life.

WHEN IT'S TIME TO STOP

One thing you know in this life is that you're going to be hurt. You are a human being, and suffering is part of your experience just as it was for Jesus. You will suffer just as surely as you breathe and eat lunch and wear clothes. You can't avoid it, but you shouldn't seek it, either. And if you have been suffering long, and have forgiven someone time and time again, or if the situation has started to endanger you in any way, there may come a time to put a stop to it.

Only you will know whether the time is ripe or not. But if you are in a self-perpetuating situation, you must ask yourself these two questions: "Is there physical danger involved?" and "Is my soul in danger?"

- God does not want an abused wife or child to accept injury time and again in the spirit of forgiveness. He wants them to have the wisdom and courage to seek spiritual and professional help.
- God does not want parents to surrender their authority to a delinquent or pushy teenager in the spirit of forgiveness. He may want them to exercise "tough love."
- God does not want shy or insecure people to accept swearing or blaspheming in their workplace in the spirit

of forgiveness. He wants them to stand up for themselves and for God and to call a halt to these indignities.

In the beautiful passage from Ecclesiastes, we remember that "There is a season for everything, a time for every occupation under Heaven":

A time for giving birth,
a time for dying;
a time for planting,
a time for uprooting what has been planted . . .
a time for healing;
a time for knocking down,
a time for building.
A time for tears,
a time for laughter;
a time for mourning,
a time for dancing . . .
A time for loving,
a time for hating;
a time for war,
a time for peace.*

There is a time to know that being tough and assertive may be the most loving, Christian act. The greatest act of mercy may be to correct an injustice, bearing in mind the future of souls.

I know quite a number of people who believe that unless they become reconciled with the person who has hurt them, they have not truly forgiven that individual. They are tormented by the separation that exists in their relationship, but the one who has offended them isn't sorry and doesn't desire reconciliation. These individuals feel very guilty over the fact that something seems to be lacking in their forgiveness. They fail to realize that repentance on the part of the offender is a prerequisite for reconciliation.

_____

*Ecclesiastes 3:1–4,8.

I am reminded of a father whose son had repeatedly stolen money from him. The father had many times actually seen the boy taking money out of his wallet, and yet when confronted with the offense, he would laugh off the accusation and say he was just taking what was rightfully his. The man wanted to forgive him and thought reconciliation would be proof of his forgiveness. But what could he do when his son refused to be reconciled? I explained to the father that it was more than enough for him to pray for his son to receive light—the light to see his wrongdoing and ask for forgiveness. By praying for his son, the father would exercise a forgiving heart and keep his own heart open for his son's future repentance. Reconciliation is something that cannot be forced. But in the meantime, he should remove his wallet and remove the temptation.

FORGIVENESS FOR YOU

For our Catholic friends, forgiveness is an act made sacred and real in the Sacrament of Reconciliation, also known as Confession. We receive the grace and healing that comes through the personal forgiveness of our sins by God through our priest. Many Catholics have lost the practice of going to Confession on a regular basis, and it is a profound loss. They run the risk of endangering their own souls, and they lose the healing power that takes place when meeting the Lord in this sacrament.

As painful as I find this situation, it is even more painful for me to realize that so many Catholics who have stopped going to church or Mass not only miss Confession, but also Holy Communion—the receiving of the Body and Blood of Jesus, which is life-giving and which enables us to persevere in our desire to be good, let alone be holy.

My Protestant friends, I'm sure, will "forgive me," but I want to digress for just a short spell and speak especially to those of you who are Catholic but who have not really been to church for a while. Maybe it's been a few years, maybe it's been a few decades, but for a lot of reasons, there are a lot of you, and I am reaching out to you at this very moment.

The Church misses you. When in your heart you stand outside the door, we know you are there and we are aching for you to come in. Maybe the Mass is different from the last time you remember it. Perhaps you don't understand the changes, or never understood the changes, and perhaps it's hard for you to feel at home.

But it is home. No matter what you have done or are doing, no matter why you left the Church or why you stopped loving the Church, the Church never stopped loving you. Your Catholic family wants and needs you.

One of the sweetest, most radiant women I've ever met came to visit us one summer. She was from southern Florida and had been a practicing Catholic since childhood. When she married in the 1950s, she gave up her faith in an effort to meet her non-Catholic husband halfway, and together they attended a non-denominational Christian church. But because neither of them was "at home" their interest in faith, and eventually God, began to wane. After their children were gone they made no pretense to attend any church at all. Sundays became just another feature of the weekend; their spirituality had been compromised to death.

Over the years, Mary was torn with a combination of guilt for abandoning her faith and a longing to return to it. But she couldn't bear the thought of walking into a confessional. "I couldn't remember what to say to the priest and I was too embarrassed to reel off a whole lifetime of sins to him, including the fact that I hadn't been in the Church for thirty years. That excuse kept me from even attending Mass," she later told me.

One weekend she was having a family reunion with her children, who are now in their twenties and thirties, and they started talking about the family graveyard and where everyone wanted to be buried.

Mary was hit hard by the truth. She knew that even though she had not lived as a Catholic, she wanted to die as one. She knew that while she could rationalize her faithlessness in life, she could not carry the lie into death. While her kids laughed and talked on into the night, Mary excused herself and went up to her room to pray. By morning, she had made the decision to go to Confession.

"It was awful, Mother. I was like an eight year old, worried about what I would say, going over a mental list of sins that went back thirty years. Thirty years! I didn't know where to begin. All I knew was that I had been living a lie and that I had to get the truth back into my life.

"I went to the parish church and the priest received me so warmly—it was as if he had been waiting for me the whole time. I told him my situation with the voice of a contrite child. And I must say that within moments, and even more so in the months that followed, I felt my dignity returning. I felt light and free. As I unburdened a lifetime of sin and then received absolution I knew I was whole again. I had let God back into my life.

"I thought the hardest part would be my husband. I expected that he would not understand my return to the Church. I figured that he would pout and consider it some kind of affront to all of our shared beliefs and convictions. But I gave him too little credit. After the first few Sundays, he started asking me about the Church, and frankly, even though at the time I didn't know much more about it than he did, it somehow brought us closer. The amazing thing is that I truly know that God has forgiven me for all the wasted years I spent away from Him. It is a miracle of grace."

Many Catholics, active and inactive alike, do not fully understand the power that resides in the Sacrament of Reconciliation or Confession. Some of us feel funny talking to the priest, as if it were the priest—not Jesus—who is forgiving our sins. When you confess to a priest and ask for absolution, you are not asking a man to forgive you. You are asking Jesus' representative on earth to listen and to be used as an instrument of God's Grace. You are confessing to Jesus. Through the priest, Jesus Himself forgives and absolves. In

Scripture, we read of Jesus speaking to the Apostles about this sacrament: "Whatever you bind on earth shall be considered bound in Heaven; whatever you loose on earth shall be considered loosed in Heaven" (Matthew 18:18). He gave the Apostles and everyone in their succession the power to be His instruments in forgiveness. He wanted you to have this chance to be healed and to <u>hear</u> the words, "I absolve you from your sins in the Name of the Father, and of the Son, and of the Holy Spirit."

"But why can't Jesus forgive me directly?" some of you ask. And it's a good question. Jesus can forgive you directly, and if you have sinned and are sincerely repentant, He will forgive you. But this is not the same thing as the healing and strengthening that results from the Sacrament of Reconciliation.

Confession is not just a matter of wiping the slate clean, although God miraculously does that, too. Confession provides you with God's Forgiveness and then some. It strengthens you so that the next time you are tempted, you will be much less likely to fall. It heals the damage that was done to your soul when you fell the first time, and it enables you to make great strides in holiness.

But to receive this grace, you must come to God with a repentant heart. In the part of the South where our monastery is, the Catholic population is rather small. I've heard that people used to tease Catholics about Saturday confessions. People thought that Catholics would breeze in on Saturday afternoon, tell their sins to the priest, and ride out into the sunset to sin all over again Saturday night. Undoubtedly, this was a bad witness and it gave rise to a lot of misunderstanding about Confession. What they failed to understand was that this type of Confession, if it occurred, was no Confession at all. Unless the person seeking the Sacrament of Reconciliation was fully repentant and determined not to repeat the sin, the Sacrament was not valid. Confession is not a game or a way to get brownie points with your spouse or God or anyone else. Confession is a powerful Sacrament of strengthening and healing.

Is it easy to bare your soul to the Lord through a priest?

No, not at all. Is it something people grow to enjoy? Usually not. But when I leave the confessional and have been absolved of my sins, I know that I have stepped closer to God and that I have pleased Him. I know that no matter what I have done, I am forgiven. I know that I have asked Him to arm me with the fortitude and strength to meet temptation head-on and overcome it. I know that He has armed me for the only battle in my life that is worthwhile, the fight to save my own soul.

In my life, I have had some exceptional confessors, but I know that everyone has not been so fortunate. If you have had a bad experience with a priest in confession, where perhaps you feel you were not understood, or when maybe he was having a bad day and cut you short—whatever human inadequacy you experienced, I pray that you do not nurse your discouragement anymore. Whatever it was, you can use it as a vehicle toward your own holiness, as painful as the problem may have been. Don't leave the Lord because of an unfortunate experience with one of His representatives. None of us is perfect, nor can we expect perfection from ourselves. Only God is perfect. And God will forgive you and give you the grace to forgive others.

TO FORGIVE IS TO BE CHRISTIAN

Granted, none of this is easy. But when we are faced with a situation that stinks, when someone has humiliated us or lied to us or struck us a blow from which we think we'll never recover, we must rise to the occasion and forgive.

God never said life was going to be one smooth sail. By the example of His Son, Our Savior, He showed us that we as Christians were almost guaranteed a rough time. He never said it would be fair or easy. But He did say that in His House were many mansions, and that one day we would be able to see the reasons and the whys for every offense and suffering.

Right now, in your pain, it might not be easy to look at the "eternal consequences" of forgiving your spouse for having an affair or forgiving a stranger for hurting your child. For all your emotions are telling you, Heaven is too far away to matter right now. You just don't care. But God isn't asking you to feel happy in the midst of your pain—He is asking you to make the difficult and unemotional decision to forgive, no matter what. You may still be deeply hurt, but you can pray for the individual who hurt you. You can only do your part, but you must <u>decide</u> to do your part.

Don't worry about the feelings that may come and go, or the events that may crop up in your memory. You are going to be tempted to hash and rehash your injury—expect that— but try to overcome it by praying for God's strength to forgive and move on. Offer your pain to God as a sacrifice, and imagine how deeply in love He is with you for giving Him the sacrifice of a broken heart. The sacrifice of one who is trying to be like God in a difficult situation is so beautiful, it causes the angels to rejoice.

Don't despair.
God believes in you.

— 8 —

Why Is It So Hard to Be Good?

OVER THE YEARS, hundreds and hundreds of priests have come through the network: some as guests, some on retreat, others just to touch base. This has been a blessing for the staff and the nuns, because we have been able to meet and to know so many extraordinary individuals. One such person was a priest from Iowa, a very gifted and popular priest who, when I first met him, was doing a lot of self-examination and renewal. Over the course of his interior pursuits, he had determined that pride, capital *P*, was stunting his spiritual growth.

"Pray for me, Mother," he said to me one afternoon. "Pray that I will receive scorn, and so be humbled before God and man."

A prayer for scorn? This was not your average prayer request. We are often asked to pray for healings, for faith, and for financial recoveries, but it is unusual for someone, even a priest, to ask us to pray for scorn. Scorn isn't just a private lesson in humiliation. Scorn is a public awareness that you are not the swell person that everyone thought you were.

Scorn is when everyone knows that you're weak, imperfect, and sinful. It's not exactly a Sunday afternoon in the park.

Nevertheless, the nuns and I duly prayed for Father's scorn that week. We didn't hear from him for about a month. When he finally called, he sounded a little distraught.

"Mother, the world has caved in all around me," he said. "I have been deluged with discontented parishioners ever since my return. I've been bungling everything I touch, and the people are complaining that I'm not running the parish right. In one month I've gone from 'Priest of the Year' to 'Father Can't-Do-Anything-Right.' "

"But Father, what did you expect?" I asked delicately. "You asked us to pray for scorn and the Lord simply answered our prayers."

"Scorn?" he said jokingly. "Where did that come from? I'm from Iowa, remember? I asked you to pray for corn, Mother. Corn."

Well, one thing the Lord didn't take away from Father was his sense of humor. Father got the scorn he asked for, in spades. Most of us don't really want such a heavy dose of self-knowledge, but self-knowledge is the key to attaining goodness (or what I prefer to call holiness) in this life. While Father experienced some pretty awful times, he also grew closer to God in his newfound humility and moved light-years forward on his spiritual journey. He rediscovered that his gifts and talents—his judgment, his charm, and his popularity—could be taken away by God just as easily as they were given to him.

"Well, that's interesting, Mother, but are you suggesting that I run out and pray for scorn tomorrow?" you ask. Not really. At least not tomorrow! But when you ask me, "Why is it so hard to be good?" my answer must center on why it is so easy to be bad. And the reason for that is simple: pride. Pride is the toughest, most subtle, insidious, and misunderstood of all the sins. It is the sin that causes us to put ourselves above God. It is the sin that confuses us and causes us to swallow lies whole—lies about ourselves and our own importance. It is the sin that caused one of the highest angels to fall and become the archenemy of God.

"Why is it so hard to be good?" The answer lies in who we think we are and who we understand God to be. For no matter what temptation we encounter, we can resist it by remembering that we are temples of the Holy Spirit. But if we put ourselves at the center of our universe and if we take credit for all the gifts God gave us as our own, we are going to sin day in and day out.

"But, Mother, I know what sin is," you insist. "I can tell when I'm true to God and when I'm really flubbing it!" That's where you've got it all wrong. Pride is a very sophisticated adversary, and its most powerful tactic is to persuade you that your own sense of sin and righteousness is an adequate or correct rule of thumb. Pride confuses us to the point that we really don't know the difference between good and evil. This is why any effort to be holy must start with the acknowledgment that you and I have much to learn about the nature of pride. We have to admit that there is a lot we don't know, and this takes a large measure of humility. We have to decide that we are dissatisfied with the conventional standards of good behavior, and that we are willing to make a gigantic leap into a territory where only saints have ventured. And to accomplish all of this, we've got to do battle with the number one impediment to self-knowledge, our own menacing pride.

GOOD PRIDE, BAD PRIDE

I probably should clarify that there are two kinds of pride, and that the first kind of pride is pretty harmless. For example, it is obviously not a sin when I say I am proud of you. It simply means that you have done something well, and that I noticed it and appreciated it.

When we say we are proud to be Americans, we are stating our deep gratitude for being citizens of this country. But if patriotism should lead to an ideology of superiority similar to Nazism, then that would be pride at its worst. This is the dangerous kind of pride—the pride that stands in the way of holiness and leads to sin because it encourages defiance of God.

Pride is the excessive self-esteem we accord ourselves from the moment we wake up to the moment we go to bed. As Saint Paul put it, "We must stop being conceited, provocative and envious. It is the people who are not important who often make the mistake of thinking that they are" (Galatians 5:26; 6:3). This pride is the pride that stops you not only from being good but also from understanding what is good.

Now I'm not trying to make you feel like a worm—far from it. What I want you to understand is that you have great dignity because you are a child of God. It's not because of who your parents are or how much money you have or because you graduated from college *summa cum laude*. These are all God's gifts to you, and not things of your own doing. It is not that these are bad things, or that you didn't have to work for them. But they are not the source of your dignity. Your true self-esteem comes from being a child of God.

The understanding of pride has eluded man since Adam and Eve. When our first parents sided with the devil, they did so out of pride. With full light—knowing all of the wretched consequences of their decision—they opted for a misleading "sense of control" over their own lives. The Genesis writer tells us that when the serpent tempted Eve to eat the fruit, he promised that she and Adam would receive ultimate knowledge of good and evil. They would be like gods, he told them, and they believed him. Adam and Eve's great sin was in choosing to assert themselves against God. They had opted for the false trinity of "me, myself, and I" at the expense of Father, Son, and Holy Spirit. Pride is one of the grave consequences of original sin, for all of us are born with prideful tendencies that cause us to be self-centered rather than God-centered.

ONE BAD APPLE

The fallout from Adam and Eve's disobedience is serious and not to be ignored. If we downplay the magnitude of original sin, we are certain to get sidetracked on our spiritual journey. The fall of Adam and Eve ensured that we, the human family, would always have a weakness for sin. Simply put, without God's Grace it is easier to say "No" to God than "Yes." I know that this is hard news, but if you can't accept this truth, it will be difficult for you to overcome the true barriers to holiness.

What is it that makes this truth hard to accept? None other than our pride, and in this case, our pride operating overtime. It is pride that tells us we are so much finer than we really are and refuses to accept that we might be wanting in some way. It is pride that prevents us from facing the reality of our weaknesses and frailties and infidelities. Pride's goal is to keep us in ignorance as long as it can. And if we habitually yield to pride, we will ultimately believe that God is superfluous to our own existence.

As Christians, we want to be holy people. Being a holy person is not just essential to our spiritual, mental, and emotional well-being; it sets the terms of our salvation. But our inner drive to be a "good person"—and to be regarded as one—is sometimes so strong that we lose our ability to judge ourselves truthfully. We settle for half-truths and fail to really scrutinize our own behavior. We let pride cover up our weaknesses. Until we can come to grips with the reality that we are weak human beings, and that we depend totally on God for everything we possess, the message of Christianity is lost on us.

"All right already, Mother! I get the point. But how can I see pride operating in my own life?" you ask. The answer is that it takes time, and a keen spiritual eye. It takes prayer, and if you ask God to help you see the pride in your life, I can promise He'll answer your petition faster than any you've ever given Him. I must confess that I spar with my own pride each and every day. For me, it has been a daily encounter because pride has so many disguises.

I'm always amused by the way the Lord works on our pride by taking us down a few pegs. I remember attending a benefit dinner in Washington, D.C., a few years ago. All the attendees were beautifully dressed in tuxedos and formal gowns, and I knew very few people there. All of a sudden a crowd of people gathered around me, all smiling, shaking my hand, and asking to have their picture taken with me. I was pleased and flattered by the attention until one gentleman clued me in on the real reason behind their warmth. "So, Mother Teresa," he said, "how are things in India?"

Being holy is doing God's Will, and sorting out His Will from your own will is no easy process. But there is one feature of pride that holds true no matter who you are or how holy you are: pride will always get you in the areas of your life that you care about most. If you want to see pride operating in your own life, look at the things you value: your family, your work, your community, and your spiritual world. And once you get attuned to looking for it, you'll find pride everywhere you look. But I need to offer a word of caution here. It's important not to get discouraged by the fact that you encounter pride so often. Rather, you can learn to use these small encounters with pride to grow in holiness and humility.

PRIDE AT HOME

Pride gets you where you live. One hard look at your home life will reveal many areas where pride has impeded your holiness and led you down the wrong path. How many times have you heard the old adage "Charity begins at home"? And yet as many times as you have heard it, the message doesn't really sink in. This is why your behavior in your home and with your family is a better measure of goodness or holiness than any other factor. The man who goes to Mass every day but spends no time with his wife is no lesson in holiness. The woman who donates forty hours a week to volunteer programs while her children stay at home with various baby-sitters is no lesson in love. And yet if you asked any of them if they felt they were serving God, they would answer with an enthusiastic "Yes." But are they?

I was in the Midwest speaking on behalf of the network recently and had the "pleasure" of dining out with an elderly couple who had done substantial fund-raising work for missionary organizations throughout Africa. Here was this hardworking Christian couple, holy by anybody's guess, locked in verbal combat all night long. It wasn't anything direct. In fact, all of the action took place in side comments. When, for example, I asked the gentleman what he did for a living, he told me he was an engineer, and then tossed out, "Not that I ever see my money, mind you. She goes through it quicker than I can make it." Undaunted, the woman simply said, "Honey, your teeth seem dirty. Isn't it time for you to go to the dentist again?" This went on all night long.

I'm sure that, had I questioned this couple about their caustic comments to each other, they would have been surprised. They probably would have assured me that they were just joking—that they hadn't meant to belittle one another. But I am continually amazed at the thoughtless ways that some spouses address each other, as if their marriage gave them license to be insulting or even rude. This is a form of pride that is particularly common but seldom acknowledged. Instead of giving their best to their spouses, people often give the scraps of their day and the scraps of their consideration.

There are pitfalls in all relationships; nobody said love was easy, and marriage is probably the toughest love of them all! But when married couples forget that faith and sacrificing for each other were a big part of their decision to marry in the first place, they give rein to their own pride and their own self-centeredness. The results, as you might guess, can be devastating.

- It is pride when a husband interrupts his wife and will not listen respectfully to her point of view, as if his opinions were the only ones worth listening to.

- It is pride if a father insists that his son become a doctor when his son has no interest in medicine and wants to become an artist.
- It is pride if a wife pushes her husband to achieve a certain level of corporate success in order to maintain a luxurious style of living.
- It is pride when a mother hesitates to correct her child under the guise of tolerance, when in reality she just doesn't want to take the risk of losing her child's love and affection.

Most of us pay little or no attention to the many thoughtless comments and gestures we make during the course of the day, but thoughtlessness is also a form of pride. It's a passive kind of pride, a pride that fails to put others first, a pride that fails to care about anyone but "Me." When a husband comes home late for dinner without calling his wife, he is displaying this kind of pride. So, too, is a child who sits down at the dinner table and complains about the food. Any time we are rude or dismissive to family members, we are failing as Christians. We are placing ourselves above another person, judging them, seeing them not as a person who is loved by God, but as a being who is somehow less important than we are. We think that our agenda is the only agenda.

"Boy, Mother, I'll never be a holy person at this rate," you say. Well, I don't believe that. I think you are well on your way to holiness because you are trying, because you are willing to open your eyes and accept some pretty brutal self-knowledge. The Lord only asks that we try, and the more we know about ourselves and our delusions, the more we can do to correct them. Self-knowledge is crucial to achieving the holiness you want in your life. When someone points out that you and I are thoughtless individuals, and that our self-absorption has taken its toll on our family life, we can begin to change. We can realize that the little things in this life matter. A modern-day spiritual writer recently pointed out that thoughtlessness is not the same as cruelty, but can often have the same effect. In our pride, we fail to see that we hurt people every day. Whenever we disregard a person's dignity by thoughtless or rude behavior, we stray from the humility that is asked of us by God.

PRIDE ON THE OUTSIDE

Pride is a problem! If pride were a person, we would see him sneaking around corners, playing tricks with mirrors and lights, trying to get us to see a world that has one lord and master: "Me." Pride would wear disguises and attack us when and where we'd least expected it, hoping we would not detect his presence. But we were not meant to spend our lifetime dodging conspiratorial forces or playing Sherlock Holmes to our pride. We were meant to be holy. And this takes practice, the hard practice of simply forgetting ourselves and thinking of God and of others.

This process of "forgetting" distinguishes the person who is merely good by conventional standards from the person who is holy. I think most of us could make the grade if holiness were just a matter of doing good deeds or being friendly to others. But it's not. Holiness is coming to realize that God is the center of our life, and acting in accordance with this tremendous truth.

You don't have to build a cathedral or fast for days or stand on street corners preaching the Word to be holy. You can do it all in your everyday life in the community, in how you handle strangers and friends, in your response to the known and the unknown. Now some of you might say "That's too easy" or "That's not enough for our Sovereign Lord." But look how we handle even the basic encounters in life:

- You are circling for a parking spot during the Christmas rush. Someone cuts in ahead of you and takes your place. You yell at the offending driver and feel tremendous rage. The driver may or may not have even known you were there. But your pride only accounts for a universe of one: you. You wonder how anyone dares to inconvenience you; your outrage is way out of proportion to the actual incident.

- You've been working late every night this week. Each morning when your secretary comes in, you throw mounds of typing down on her desk and brusquely order her to take care of it, never thanking her or showing common courtesy. Your pride has told you that you are the only one in the world who works late, and somehow, she and the rest of the office are to blame for this. Your self-centeredness lowers her morale and self-esteem.

- A beggar on the street approaches you. You are repulsed by him, but, prompted by Christian duty, you shove a dollar into his hand. Your pride tells you how wonderful you are, but the rude manner in which you helped this man did not add to his dignity; it lowered it.

- You are a doctor or a lawyer. A client comes in with a problem. He is slow to understand your diagnosis, and you are impatient with him and flood him with medical or legal jargon. Your pride has told you that he is not equipped to understand much anyway, and that your time is more important than his, so you intimidate him right out of the office.

- You are standing in line waiting to pay for your groceries. The elderly person in front of you is having a hard time piecing together her correct change. You shift from one leg to the other, and sigh loudly in exasperation. Your pride has told you that the world should be accommodating you and never vice versa.

If this sounds like I am just telling you to mind your p's and q's, I'm not. What I am trying to do is to clear up the way you think about yourself in the world. You're not such a big wheel. You're just a cog in it. Every time you exert superiority or condescension over someone else, you have fallen into pride. Whether you are griping at a rotten driver or criticizing your spouse in public or treating a waiter like a slave, you have assaulted the dignity of someone whom God loves very much. These assaults reflect our weakness of vision, our failure to have compassion, and the self-centeredness that flaws our holiness. Taken one at a time, I guess these episodes don't amount to much. But when they begin to accumulate, pride can leave you in a lonely world with a population of one.

PRIDE VERSUS GOD

The pitfalls that pride creates for us are many and varied. One of pride's greatest tricks is to use complacency to stunt our understanding of holiness. Pride deceives us into believing that we don't need to grow beyond the simple black-and-white understandings we were given as children, the "do's and don't's" that many of us have carried into adulthood. All of us are victimized by this mind-set. We firmly believe that "being good" is simply a matter of following the rules. We obey the Commandments, we go to church on Sunday, we give to charities and make soup for a sick neighbor every now and then. As long as we keep up this effort, we feel satisfied. After all, we're not cheating on our spouse, right? We put a few dollars into the collection plate, don't we? What more does God want, anyway?

Complacency is our pride busy at work. I am reminded of a story told to me by the pastor of a small church outside of Boston. It is about a middle-aged man who used to run into Mass every day for about two minutes. The man would scramble into the church, kneel down in a pew, pray a couple of minutes, jump up, and run out again. All the pious ladies in the church used to turn and scowl at him, and even the priest scratched his head now and then, wondering just what this man was up to.

One day the pastor grabbed the man on his way out and said, "Sir, may I ask why you scramble in and out of our church every day? You really ought to stay for the full Mass, you know." The man explained that he was a train engineer, and that he only had a few minutes to stop in the town. "But what could you possibly pray for in just a few minutes?'' the pastor asked. "I don't pray for anything, really," the man shrugged. "I just say 'Hello, Jesus, this is Jim.' "

A short time later, there was a train collision and the pastor was called to the local hospital to minister to the victims. One of the injured men was Jim. He was dying. The priest talked to him for a few minutes, then gave him the Last Rites. Suddenly the pastor heard a voice.

"Hello, Jim," the Voice said softly. "This is Jesus."

This story can teach us a lot about ourselves. Most of us, I'm afraid, are like the pious ladies in the pews. Our pride tells us that there is a correct way to worship God, and by golly, that's that. We think that by following the rules we are being "good," and our pride tells us that others should follow our example. But the Lord sees things differently. He saw that Jim's faith was in his heart, and that the effort Jim made every day increased his love for God. If we judge Jim or are disdainful of his style or if we begrudge him a place in the Mass, then we have strayed from the path of goodness. Our pride has confused the issue once again.

I guess that, for obvious reasons, spiritual pride is one of the most dangerous of all forms of pride. I often see people judging others for their apparent lack of gifts, whether spiritual or intellectual. They have missed the point of those gifts entirely. The nature of gifts is that they are given. Every talent and strength and bit of wisdom comes from God, not from one's ancestry or some intense training program.

A story about two monks who lived in the fourteenth century illustrates my point. The two monks were Franciscans, like the nuns and me. One of them was simple, what you might call a nobody. He was always bungling his prayers and speaking at the wrong moment. He had unpleasant ways and his habit was always askew. No one much liked him. The other monk was reputed to be an accomplished Franciscan scholar. He was erudite, a brilliant thinker, and people flocked from miles around to hear his wisdom.

Oddly, the two of them died on the same day, and were buried shortly thereafter. The first monk's funeral was spare and perfunctory, and attended only by the abbot and the friars.

The second monk's funeral was solemn and grand, and it was attended by townsfolk and clergy from all over the city. But on the night the two were buried, the abbot had a strange dream. In his dream, he saw the simple monk smiling lovingly upon him from Heaven. He was surrounded by angels, praising God. The second monk was burning in hell. "How could this be?" the abbot wondered, even in his dream. God then revealed to him that the scholar had always been motivated by pride, by the favor of men, and by the honors and the accolades he had received. The scholar had believed his wisdom was his own, rather than a gift from God. He had never truly loved God, for he was too busy loving himself. He had subscribed to the lie of pride, and was suffering the consequences.

I think that God is most hurt by the pride that contaminates the spiritual world, because it affects those who, at one point at least, were so close to achieving holiness. When He sees some so-called Christian warriors looking down upon those who are not Christian or reveling in a certain smugness that they know something others don't know, He must be very pained. Jesus warned us of the dangers of this kind of prideful behavior in the parable about the Pharisee and the publican.

The Pharisee, as you recall, passed a publican (a tax collector) in the back of the temple. The publican was beating his breast in sorrow for his sins. But the Pharisee went up to the altar and said, "Thank you, God, that I am not grasping, unjust, adulterous like the rest of mankind, and particularly that I am not like this tax collector here. I fast twice a week; I pay tithes on all I get." The Pharisee was extolling his spiritual virtues, but it is clear that his spiritual conceit knew no bounds.

The Pharisee's behavior was prideful in two respects. Not only did he look down on the publican in condescending judgment, but even worse, he gave himself credit for what God had given him. His prayer was not a prayer of thanksgiving to God, but one that seemed to expect God to thank him. The Lord condemned the behavior of the Pharisee, but the publican, who considered himself a poor sinner, won

God's favor because of his humble repentance (Luke 18:9–14).

There is another kind of spiritual conceit that displeases God, and that is apparent in the person who spends a lot of time visiting prisons, taking care of the elderly, and witnessing to others while his family sits at home alone and neglected. This person is overzealous, determined to save the world. He forgets that Jesus has already saved the world. He may be sincere, but he has fallen, once again, for the lie of pride. And in the process he wounds the ones he is supposed to love the most.

You may be saying, "Oh, come on, Mother, doesn't his sincerity count for something?" Sure it does. But it's like the time I planned to fly to New York. I arrived at the airport and proceeded to board the plane. Imagine my surprise when the flight attendant announced after takeoff that the plane would arrive on schedule in Miami, Florida. I was sincere in boarding the plane, but I was sincerely wrong as to which plane I had boarded.

Please understand. There is nothing wrong with the man wanting to do good things for God. But when those things begin to interfere with his first responsibility, to care for his family, then he needs to reassess his priorities.

Clearly, this business of holiness is not as easy as it seems. Holiness asks us to go beyond rules and regulations and everything we ever thought was "good behavior." It asks us to face ourselves squarely, to pursue the kind of self-knowledge that will transform our existence from the merely mundane to the decidedly divine.

PRIDE AND POSITIVE THINKING

Spiritual pride is as old as the hills, but there is also a modern-day pride, a pride that manifests itself under the giant umbrella of "positive thinking," and we should confront it. Although it is important for us to have a certain degree of self-confidence, I've found that at the core of the positive thinking philosophy is an attitude that encourages pride. It is with this point that I seriously differ.

One of my primary objections to the positive thinking philosophy is that it perpetuates the notion that God loves most those who are healthy, wealthy, and wise. Positive thinkers seem to lack an understanding that followers of Jesus must be willing to take up their cross daily, and that those who do not enjoy health and prosperity are often among God's most beloved chosen ones. Because positive thinkers focus on happiness or material goods and worldly comforts, they often miss the freedom that comes with living in the present moment and being able to accept the Will of God, even if it means suffering.

It really grates on my nerves when someone is eating a plate of beans and he tries to insist that they taste like chicken. Beans are beans, my friend, and they don't taste like chicken. I believe it's far better to simply accept the fact that you're eating beans, and thank God for what you've got.

When you subscribe to "positive thinking" you put all of your chips on how you <u>want</u> to feel today. You lose your job through your own negligence or indifference and try to turn that into a positive: "It was a rotten job anyway; I'll just go get a new and better one." You lied to your spouse: "Golly, that wasn't nice of me; I'll just take her out to dinner and we'll be happier than ever." Because you can't accept the situation for what it is, you think that every little problem can be corrected by seeing the good—if only the imagined good—in a situation and taking a "positive" action upon it.

What happens to your soul in the meantime? You have avoided thinking about why you lost your job or lied to your wife. You have kept God out of the process entirely by not asking Him for help or forgiveness. You have presumed that all the forces at work in this world are shallow, human forces. But your response is an equally shallow, ever-cheerful outlook that supports only one person's happiness: yours.

If the emphasis is on your happiness, then self-knowledge becomes a problem. Self-knowledge typically does not make one happy. In fact, it's usually pretty grim stuff. But, grim or not, self-knowledge is at the root of Christian transformation. And this transformation relies on your cooperation with God, not your inner reserve or any delusion that you alone can pull yourself out of the mess you're in.

This is why I believe that Christians can embrace positive thinking only when the "positive" is God. Our objective in this life is not to have a fixed grin on our face all the time. We are not guaranteed a life without pain. On the contrary— our model, Jesus Christ, lived a life of suffering. He didn't have to start His day with a pep rally, nor did He indulge in mental gymnastics to get pumped up in the morning. He just asked the Father for help, in utter humility, knowing that whatever happened would be the Father's Will. Jesus was the example of perfect liberty, because He accepted whatever it was that the Father wanted for Him.

PRIDE AND THE FALSE MARTYR

In the end, we cannot understand pride without understanding the humility of Jesus. When we talk about examples in which pride has tainted our behavior, we can easily confuse the proper response, which is humility, with the improper response, which is the old doormat routine. This is why I am compelled to repeat constantly: Christians are not doormats. Christians are children of God, who are humbled by that very fact. When the waiter brings the wrong order to our table, we would be crazy to think that the humble response is to eat it and so avoid hurting the waiter's feelings. That response would be just as prideful as the response that has us screaming at the poor guy. Meekly accepting the wrong food involves a fastidiousness and a false cross that focuses, again, on us. As a matter of fact, once we bite into that hamburger that is not ours, we have really messed things up for the waiter, because the guy whose hamburger we are "meekly" munching is probably throwing a fit over our crab claws!

So don't confuse self-imposed crosses and contrived martyrdom with humility. Both, I'm sorry to say, are functions of pride. When we let people bully us or beat up on us, we allow them to hurt someone God loves very much—namely, us. But that's not where it ends. Because if you facilitate another person's sin, you enable him to damage his own soul, and this was not your point at all. Humility is not wearing a "kick me" sign; it is simply putting God first. It is keeping a perspective on the events of daily life and opting for the holy choice in the present moment, no matter what the circumstances.

I remember a woman who came to me very distraught several years ago. Anna had been suffering verbal and emotional abuse from her husband for a number of years. He constantly belittled her, and by the time she came to see me she was convinced that she was a failure—with her husband, with her children, with her life.

I asked her to describe a typical day.

"It starts from the time we get up in the morning until we go to sleep," she said. "He doesn't like the way I cook, the way I clean the house, or the way the children behave. My work is unimportant to him. No matter what I do, it's never right."

"Does he ever hit you?" I asked.

"No."

"Have you tried to discuss the problem with him?"

"Oh, no," Anna replied. "I could never do that. He gets too angry. I just can't take his yelling and complaining anymore."

"Then tell him," I said.

She looked at me in horror.

"I'm serious," I continued. "When he comes home tonight, the moment he begins to complain about dinner, calmly inform him where he can find the nearest restaurant. And every time he starts yelling, let him know that he can go or you can go, but that you and your children are going to live in peace."

"But I could never . . ."

"Look," I said. "It is not God's Will for you to live in this kind of turmoil. You're not helping anybody by remaining silent and simply taking all this abuse. Is what you've got to lose worse than what you're going through now?"

Anna looked at me—unconvinced. She left the monastery shaking her head.

But she called the following week.

"Mother, you were right!" she said. "It worked!"

She proceeded to tell me how she had finally stood up for herself and for her children. Each time her husband began to complain, she would calmly but firmly let him know what he could do with his complaints. Within a week the situation had changed dramatically. Anna's husband was developing a new-found respect for her, and Anna was beginning to believe more in herself, too.

I need to stress at this point that my advice to Anna was based upon the fact that there was no physical abuse in their marriage. Anna's husband was simply a proud man who tried to raise himself up by putting down his wife and children. But to those who are encountering physical abuse, you are facing an entirely different set of circumstances. The person who is abusing you is not suffering simply from pride, but from a deep-seated illness. In such cases extensive counseling from a qualified professional is required.

I am also not suggesting for a moment that Anna's situation happens only to women. I've seen any number of wives who belittle their husbands so badly that the poor men dread coming home at night.

What I'm saying is that God made families to be living symbols of His Love. He did not design the home to be a battleground. And while I do not advocate divorce, neither do I believe in women or men being passive victims of another's abuse. Often those who remain passive and silent mistake their meekness for virtue, when instead it is weakness cloaked in fear.

Humility is a challenge, isn't it? It calls for us to return, over and over again, to God as the center of our lives. We will always get caught in traps of self-absorption, and most of our lives we will waver between thinking we are the big cheese and believing we are the scum of the earth. But we must remember that our God loves us and, as Christians, we are bound to uphold each other's dignity as children of God.

PRIDE AND FREEDOM

You and I are poor, frail human beings just trying to do the best we can. We want to be good, but our pride keeps whispering lies to us, keeping the focus on ourselves rather than on God. In the grips of our own pride, we can come to believe the ultimate falsehood, that freedom is a condition apart from God rather than the state of being united to His Will.

If we are attuned to God's Will, then when we sin, we do not experience an immediate sense of release or freedom. We feel guilt. We scream at a co-worker and then spend the rest of the afternoon regretting our action. We steal a client away from a partner and then become preoccupied with how we can help him make up the loss of income. And yet our culture, which places so much stock in the Marlboro man, the strong, independent, self-sufficient individual, has a tough time accepting the idea that we might need anybody, least of all a Creator Whom we cannot even see. We think that strength comes in believing we can stand on our own, rather than in accepting the only force that can keep us up. We nurture our own pride and in so doing we falter on the path to holiness, when just one Truth could change our entire lives.

This one Truth, of course, is Jesus. As much as you'd prefer to do it all on your own, you've got to follow Him if you seek salvation. This is no slight on you. We are not for a moment disputing the fact that you are an intelligent, talented, beautiful human being. Following Jesus doesn't take away from you, it makes you possible. The key lies in understanding that everything wonderful and good in you is not because of you, but because God decided to give it to you.

"Why is it so hard to be good?" The answer remains that we are all stained by original sin and a legacy of pride. We are all tempted to believe that we are the one, when He is the One. Our pride leads us away from self-knowledge, the knowledge without which we cannot become the extraordinary child of God whom He meant us to be.

Pride leads man to sin in the pursuit of his own goals, and

that is why pride is such a ruthless adversary. Pride will sneak up on you when your intentions are at their very best and when you want more than anything else to do the right thing. If you are not aware of your own pride at work, it can truly be your downfall. If you happen to be wrestling with a particular sin, a habitual sin, your own weakness, or if you have reached a plateau or level of lukewarmness in your spiritual life, ask God to make you aware of the pride in your life. Ask Him to show you where you have put yourself before Him, and you will begin to make tremendous breakthroughs in your family relationships, your spiritual life, your community life, and your own sense of who you are and why you are. Above all, and especially if you are wrestling with a sin, be honest with God, your Father. If we refuse to admit our failings before God, we are truly in a sorry state. For if we cannot be honest with Someone Who sees everything we do, who will we be honest with?

Father Frederick W. Faber said, "To attack other men's faults is to do the devil's work; to do God's work is to attack our own." If you want to be holy, if you seek meaning in your life, start looking into your own life and attacking your pride in all of its many forms. God will give you extraordinary light and the ultimate reward of holiness. For your holiness relies not on what you do, but on what you allow God to do through you.

Have courage.
God will perfect you.

Part III

LAST THINGS

— 9 —

Must I Believe in Guardian Angels, Saints, and Purgatory Too?

A YOUNG FRIEND dropped by the monastery one afternoon and confessed that he had reached an impasse on a subject very dear to my heart. Angels. "I just can't believe all of that angels stuff, Mother," Thomas confided. "Isn't it enough to believe Jesus is Lord? Do I have to buy all of those flying cherubs, too?"

Flying cherubs, my eye. Clearly, Thomas needed to learn a thing or two about some of his dearest friends. And so, after a lengthy discussion during which he was mostly silent, the young man heard more about angels than he had ever bargained for. He left unconvinced, and for some reason I did not expect to hear from him anytime soon, although I knew that our paths would cross again.

Sure enough, about a year later, Thomas called from a telephone booth at the Birmingham airport. He had just returned from Rome and wanted to see me at once. Within minutes, he was sitting in our parlor on the edge of his chair, with the wild-eyed look of a man who had just seen a ghost.

"Mother," he said hoarsely, "you weren't kidding!"

"About what?" I asked hesitantly.

"About the angels, of course! They are real," he said excitedly. "Last week, I was walking out of St. Peter's after Confession," he said breathlessly, "and I felt as happy as a man could be. I wandered through the hundreds of people in the square, crossed the street to wait for a bus, and suddenly became aware of something bright beside me.

"Well, it was a gorgeous day, and I thought the sunlight was reflecting strangely on some passersby, or that someone was wearing an exotic costume. Only I was wrong. It was a beautiful angel with a serene smile on his face. I tried to get hold of my senses—you know what a skeptic I am, Mother—but no matter what I did, I could not escape this creature.

"I was starting to get nervous. Then I looked back at Saint Peter's Square and it was apparent that everyone had his own angel. I panicked. I stepped into the bus and looked around fearfully, only to see more angels. Four or five kids were cutting up in the back of the bus and their angels were frolicking above them in the luggage rack. Two older ladies were gossiping and their angels looked sad. When I looked out the window, I saw an old drunk sitting on the curb, and his angel had his arm around the man's shoulder, trying to comfort him.

"I just couldn't take any more. I got off the bus at the next stop and ran back to my confessor as fast as I could. When I asked him what it all meant, he shrugged and said it simply meant that I was wrong about angels, and that God wanted me to know they were real.

"Mother, I take back everything I ever said about you and your love for the angels. We really do have angels," Thomas said with a sigh. "And they are as real as you and me."

Well, I could have saved Thomas the price of a round-trip ticket to Rome for that little bit of insight, but sometimes the Lord wants us to see things firsthand. For Thomas, like his "doubting" namesake, seeing was believing. Thomas was given this extraordinary vision because he wanted to understand so urgently the truth about angels, and it's clear that God was very touched by his thirst to know.

Most people, however, couldn't care less. They think that angels are for children or, at best, for somebody else. They are content to ignore a gigantic aspect of our universe just because they can't see it. And so, over the past centuries, angels have been relegated to the status of some kind of fantastic oddity, like unicorns or goblins or UFOs. I find this attitude, among other things, terribly rude. I find it appalling that there are millions of spirits fighting our battles and praying for our souls while we blithely ignore them or treat them like some kind of tooth fairies.

The truth is that angels are as real as we are, and we know this because God revealed it to us. And I will also tell you that there is at least one angel who cares about you very much.

WHAT ARE ANGELS?

When I casually mention my guardian angel to Catholic and Protestant friends, I often find myself in the middle of an eyebrow-raising contest. It doesn't take a mind reader to know what they're thinking. Usually, it's something like "I'll just stay quiet and humor her" or "I'm sure she meant to say God." Meanwhile, their brains are filled with images of fat little children with curly hair and wings. "How could anyone really believe in angels?" they whisper to themselves.

The answer to that is simple. People believe in angels because angels exist. Angels aren't cute, chubby little cherubs. When you confine your thinking to the ornaments on top of Christmas trees and images on Italian frescoes, you can rightfully conclude that such is the stuff of artists' imaginations. But if your thinking stops there, you are guilty of intellectual shortsightedness. Worse, you insult one winged creature in particular, who will remain nameless because you probably haven't even given him a name! The fact is that you do have your own angel, a guardian angel, who is pleased as punch that you are reading about him right now. And no matter what you've heard to the contrary, I am telling you in the tradition of the Church, Saint Thomas Aquinas, and all of Scripture that there are angels everywhere in the universe.

"But what is an angel, Mother?" you ask. "If they aren't little cupids, how am I supposed to picture them?" Well, the word "angel" actually means "messenger," but that is a designation of mission rather than nature. By nature angels are pure spiritual and intellectual beings, and when I say pure, I mean one hundred percent. They can be joyful, sorrowful, compassionate; indeed, they can manifest unique personalities, just like human beings. But they are in no way material. This is why we shouldn't get hung up on mental pictures if we can avoid them.

YOUR GUARDIAN ANGEL

These amazing creatures whom we ignore or make fun of are specifically mentioned by Jesus in Saint Matthew's Gospel. In Matthew 18:10, Jesus scolds the Apostles for complaining about the little children crowding around Him. He says to them, "See that you never despise any of these little ones, for I tell you that their angels in Heaven are continually in the Presence of My Father." And yet we continue to believe that angels don't exist. The odd thing about this "angel abuse" is that we have more in common with angels than any other creatures in the universe. Like angels, we are intelligent beings. We were created to praise God, to glorify Him, and to be with Him in Heaven.

Now I know what many of you are thinking. You're thinking, "Mother, this is just too weird." You can't handle the notion that there are millions of spirits out there, all of whom are brighter than you are. You're back on the wings and chubby faces again, and you just can't accept it.

Well, I can't give you charts and proofs and scientific samples of angels' wings, nor would I ever presume it possible. But the Scriptures are full of examples of how God has used angels to intervene in the lives of men and women. If you have accepted the reality of God on faith, then you have already made a leap of such proportion that accepting the reality of angels should actually be simple. But whether you believe in angels or not, whether you realize that you have your own guardian angel or not, your angel—unsung hero that he is—has done a lot for you since your conception and will continue to do so every moment of your existence.

- He warns you. Sometimes what we call "intuition" leads us to make what turn out to be important decisions. You get the nagging feeling that you should not attend a certain party or that you should pick up your kids early, and while you won't always know it at the time, your guardian angel has helped you to avert danger.
- He inspires you. When you are facing a temptation of some kind and suddenly find the presence of mind to say "No," it is often your guardian angel at work, trying to gently lead you away from sin.
- He prays for you. Your guardian angel prays for you constantly. In the Book of Tobit (which is in the Catholic Bible), Tobias' angel told him, "When you prayed, I brought your prayers to the Most High" (Tobit 12:12). All of our prayers reach the Father, of course, but your angel delivers them specially.
- He gives you light. Sometimes, when you're trying to make a decision, you'll get a last-minute insight that makes everything clear to you. It's as if a piece of the puzzle had been missing, and now everything makes sense.

Guardian angels can intervene in our lives as long as their request is consistent with the Will of God. They can and do wage battles to help us when we least expect it.

I will never forget an incident that happened when I was

ten or eleven years old. I was still living in Canton, Ohio, and had gone to the town square in the early evening to run some errands for my mother. There was a parking lot in the middle of the square, and for some reason it was blocked off by a big chain that day so cars could not enter. I blithely strolled across the street when I suddenly heard someone screaming, and I looked around only to see a pair of headlights coming at me. I was temporarily blinded, and then felt two hands pick me up and swing me over the chain barricade.

The car had run a red light and sped on. Slowly, I realized what had happened. Dozens of people ran up to ask how I had leaped over the chain. I had no idea how I had gotten there.

I ran home and burst into the house looking for my mother. I was pale and trembling and started crying. "Mother, I almost got killed tonight." Then she, too, started crying and said, "I know, Rita, I know."

Later, I learned that my mother had sensed somehow that I was in danger earlier that afternoon and had knelt down to pray, asking God to save my life. Clearly, God had sent my angel to do just that. I will never forget that odd sensation of being lifted, literally lifted, by two hands over a chain that separated me from death.

You and I and everyone who ever lived all have guardian angels. They are powerful friends, probably the most powerful friends you will ever have. I don't know about you, but I've always needed all the friends I could get, and therefore have been on very close terms with my angel since the day of the near-tragedy. I call my angel Fidelis, which is Latin for faithful, and faithful he has been, for I know I've been a tough assignment.

So whether you have a hard time acknowledging your angel or not, ask him to pray for you the next time you're ill. If you're a student, ask him to help you concentrate on your next exam. If you're a salesman, ask him to help you before your next big sales call. And if you're a parent, ask the guardian angel of your son and daughter to protect your children every day of their lives.

God loves you so much that He gave you a guardian angel

a friend who prays for you, cheering you on, concerned for your salvation. If you've ever been overcome by loneliness, you should remember the friend God has given you as part of your birthright. He is with you every moment of the day.

We should always keep in mind that God never made us to be alone. We might be sitting in an empty room, we might feel abandoned and deserted and unloved, but with us right now is an angel, whose whole mission in life is to protect us. Above us and around us are all of those who've gone before us, and this angel, this beautiful angel, who is constantly fighting spiritual battles in our name.

We are not alone.

If ever you wanted a friend who understood, and who accepted you for what you were; if ever you wanted a person who was not disheartened about your weaknesses or your sins; if ever you wanted someone who would pray for you no matter what, you've got him. You've got a guardian angel. In the Mass for the Feast of the Archangels, we pray: "God our Father . . . may those who serve you constantly in Heaven keep our lives safe from all harm on earth." With the millions of angels who are praying for you now, and a guardian angel who cares especially for you, you should never feel afraid.

FRIENDS IN HIGH PLACES

Not only do you have a guardian angel, but you have a whole host of saints who pray for you now. These saints are souls who have been judged worthy to live with God in Heaven. As Catholics, we describe this powerful presence as the Communion of Saints. A lot of my Protestant friends think that we Catholics "worship" the saints, but that's not it at all. As Catholics, we ask the saints to pray for us, just as I might ask you to pray for me or for the network.

The Communion of Saints has always been very easy for me to accept. Aside from the numerous references to the saints in Scripture, it only seems logical to acknowledge that the saints perform specific work in Heaven. An important part of that work is intercessory prayer.

Perhaps people have such a hard time envisioning the saints interceding for us because we focus too much on the death of the body. When those we love depart and we can no longer see them and talk to them audibly, we tend to feel they are no longer a part of our lives. While we may direct comments toward them, we often feel foolish doing it. We don't hear a response, so we dismiss our efforts as futile.

But to "give up" on those in Heaven is a big mistake. Because those who have "made it," those who kneel before the Throne of God, are in a far better position to ask God for help on our behalf than anyone who's still living on earth.

The Book of Revelation paints a vivid picture of the Communion of Saints. It illustrates that we are one big family, some of us "there" and some of us here.

> *I, John, saw a huge number, impossible to count, of people from every nation, race, tribe and language; they were standing in front of the Throne and in front of the Lamb (Jesus), dressed in white robes and holding palms in their hands. They shouted aloud, "Victory to our God, Who sits on the Throne, and to the Lamb!" And all the angels who were standing in a circle round the Throne, prostrated themselves before the Throne, and touched the ground with their foreheads, worshipping God with these words, "Amen. Praise and glory and wisdom and thanksgiving and honour and power and strength to our God for ever and ever. Amen" (Revelation 7:9–12).*

The saints are men and women who have experienced the same miseries, heartaches, and traumas that you and I experience. Most of them lived in obscurity during their lives on earth. They were ordinary people who fought the good fight. They understand our weaknesses and struggles; they give us courage to carry on. Their friendship enhances our spiritual life and gives us a sense of companionship. Reading their lives inspires us to strive for holiness. And asking their intercession gives us a sense of family and assurance.

As you know, I've always been a saint-watcher. I am amazed at the way various saints responded to God's grace. They are extraordinary examples of ordinary human beings who struggled with their sins and overcame them. Matt Talbot was an alcoholic who became a man of prayer and penance. Saint Jerome, who had a terrible temper, struggled hard to become gentle. Mary of Egypt was a prostitute at age sixteen. She converted, became a hermit, and was known for her holiness. There were saints who did the impossible, like Mother Cabrini, who founded sixty-two schools, hospitals, and orphanages, one for every year she lived, even though she suffered from continual bouts with malaria. There were saints who were illiterate, like Catherine of Siena, who later became a Doctor of the Church. Saint Bonaventure and Saint Thomas Aquinas had great intellects. Saint Francis, the saint in rags whom I follow, gave up a comfortable life to become holy.

When we as Catholics sit before a statue of Mary or Saint Anthony or Saint Joseph, we are not worshiping a piece of marble or concrete. We are looking at an image of someone whom we love deeply, much as we would gaze lovingly at a photograph of a dear family member. Whenever we are in need, we can turn to these saints, who hear us and pray for us and make special petitions for us to the Father. And so we should never ignore these friends, noble and good, whom God in His Mercy has given us.

A DETOUR AFTER DEATH

In discussing the elements of the next world, I would be remiss if I didn't include Heaven, hell, and Purgatory. Since they are final destinations of the spiritual journey, I've written separate chapters on Heaven and hell. But the remaining place, Purgatory, isn't like Heaven or hell. Purgatory is not a destination, but a place of passage, a way station if you will, on the journey to Heaven.

Each soul is judged by God at the moment of death. The soul who has been faithful to God throughout life and has been transformed into the Image of Jesus will at death find eternal rest in Heaven. But for most of us, our lives have been filled with times when we chose what we wanted to do rather than what God wanted us to do. We haven't totally rejected God, but neither have we been entirely faithful to Him. We are burdened with the excess baggage of selfishness, envy, anger, or resentment.

If our soul is in this state, we are not prepared to live with God in Heaven. Especially not if some of the people we refused to forgive are already there. For Heaven to be a place of eternal peace and everlasting joy, something has to change. And that something is the state of our soul. At this point, it is imperative that we understand:

Death only <u>separates</u> the soul from the body. It does not <u>change</u> the soul.

At death, our will is set. All our choices have already been made. When we understand this truth, we take an important step in understanding the need for Purgatory. Because the soul cannot change after death, there is no opportunity to ask God's forgiveness when we face Him in judgment. It is not a question of suddenly realizing all our sins and begging God for mercy. "I'm sorry, I'm sorry, I'm sorry" won't alter the fact that our soul is ill-prepared to face God, let alone live with Him in Heaven.

This is where Purgatory comes in. For the first time, the soul sees itself as God sees it. It is painfully aware of its sins and weaknesses, of all the times it failed to imitate Jesus. It knows that it is not ready to gaze upon the Perfect God, since it is not perfect. Instead, the soul must be purified before it can withstand the sight of God.

Consider the sun as an example. We all know that to look directly at the sun can cause permanent damage to our eyes, even blindness. It is necessary to prepare the eyes by using the proper protective devices. Without these measures, we are not equipped to see the brilliance of the sun. Our eyes simply don't have what it takes to withstand the light.

So it is with Purgatory. The soul that is not like Jesus must be prepared before it can face God. It must be purified, purged of the sins and weaknesses that make it unable to see the glory of God.

I know that many people have a hard time with the notion of Purgatory. They insist that the Merciful God forgives sins; that He wants us to be saved. That is absolutely true. But it is also true that God is just. His Justice demands that souls be judged according to the ways in which they chose to follow His Will in this life. It is not reasonable to think that God would judge someone whose whole life was dedicated to serving Him in the same manner as someone who just wanted to "get by."

An example of this is found in Saint Luke's Gospel, where Jesus encourages us to be ready when He calls us. He speaks at length about the servant who is prepared when his master returns. He says at one point,

> *The servant who knows what his master wants, but has not even started to carry out those wishes, will receive very many strokes of the lash. The one who did not know, but deserves to be beaten for what he has done, will receive fewer strokes (Luke 12:47—48).*

This passage raises the question of how the punishment, or strokes of the lash, will be administered. They cannot be given in Heaven, since Heaven is a place without pain or suffering. And they can't be administered in hell, since hell is a place of no return.

Then how could this punishment take place? Let me first state that I prefer the word purification to punishment. I believe that Purgatory exists because we place ourselves there. Our souls are in need of cleansing in order to be able to live with God. And our sorrow over offending Him, coupled with a burning desire to be with Him, constitutes our purification, our Purgatory.

It is good for us to think about the next life, about the

spiritual world that we cannot see, hear, or touch. It is good for our souls to realize that our journey isn't over yet—but we don't know how far away we are from its end. Our lifetime journey may go on for a long time, or it may be over sooner than we think. That's why it's so important to use every means at our disposal to grow in holiness, to prepare and strengthen our souls for that moment of meeting our Creator. Angels and saints alike can help us to join their ranks, to reach our final goal of Heaven.

God wants <u>you</u> to be in that number.
When the saints go marching in.

—10—

Why Am I Afraid to Die?

A S AN INDEPENDENT SORT OF CHILD, I had a problem with my academic career. Namely, teachers. Sixth grade was particularly troublesome. No matter what I did, I could not please my teacher, Sister Prudence. She was not a woman to hide her feelings and it seemed like I was always suffering her private disapproval, which was not easy, or her public scorn, which was unjust.

After months of gritting my teeth in silence, I chose to take a different approach and make my name as a "good student." I decided I would go the Thomas Aquinas route to Heaven, since I had blown it as a Little Flower and didn't have the temperament for a Joan of Arc. Brains. That's how I would get there. I applied my every waking moment to study. It was springtime, nearing Holy Week, and I remember preparing for my catechism class. The question for the day was about death. After some opening remarks, Sister asked, "Children, can anyone tell me what the opposite of death is?"

Not one child stirred. Anyone could have seen that this

was a trick question, but I was determined to please. My hand shot up to the heavens.

"Yes, Rita?" she said with an arched brow.

"The opposite of death is life," I responded primly.

"If the opposite of death is life, then I might as well hang up my habit and join the circus," Sister Prudence said with a frown.

Obviously, my answer was incorrect. It was years before I understood why.

Most of our fears about death arise from the simplistic perception that death is the opposite of life. The very thought of death makes us depressed and discouraged. We envision everything that is dear to us coming to an end. Perhaps we even contemplate the "futility of it all." Well, if death truly were the opposite of life (as I might have led you to believe fifty years ago), we'd have every reason to despair. It would mean that a lot of us, like all of Christianity and Western civilization, are wrong. It would mean that my vows were wasted breath and that goodness was an illusion and that Jesus' coming to save us was in vain. Every bit of our understanding of right and wrong would be a joke if death were the opposite of life.

I'm aware that these are broad and sweeping statements, but unless we understand that only our <u>bodies</u> die, and that our souls continue to live forever, then everything we do and believe in this life is pointless and without worth. It is as Saint Paul says in his first letter to the Corinthians: "If there is no resurrection of the dead, Christ Himself cannot have been raised, and if Christ has not been raised, then our preaching is useless and your believing it is useless. If our hope in Christ has been for this life only, we are the most unfortunate of all people" (1 Corinthians 15:13–14, 19).

The problem with my answer to Sister Prudence was that death doesn't <u>have</u> an opposite. Death is a transition. It is no more the opposite of life than a bridge is the opposite of the land it connects. As Christians, we realize that the soul is breathed into the natural body at conception, animates the body until physical death, and then continues its life journey to eternity. Death is the death of the body, but not the soul. Death is merely a station on the way. If we could get a glimpse of the eternal nature of our lives, we would view death exactly as we view birth: a necessary tunnel through which we must pass on our journey.

Does this make it easier to face our own death or to handle the loss and separation of loved ones who die? Not really. Accepting the death of our bodies is always going to be hard, but understanding it is crucial to an informed, intelligent view of existence. If we come to understand death for what it really is, you and I can expand our knowledge of God's Plan and increase our own stamina in the pursuit of holiness. The key is to grasp that death is a fact of life, but not the end of life.

FROM HERE TO THERE

We live in a temporary city. Everything about our existence conspires to reveal the truth: that this life is a passing, fleeting moment on our way to eternity.

- We look in the mirror every day and see a different person, with new wrinkles, sagging expressions, and declining abilities.
- We strive for promotions and bigger houses, and the moment we secure them we find ourselves chasing even bigger dreams.
- We see well-known people rise and fall in momentary successes and failures, and we see the transient nature of worldly achievements.

The rewards of this life are elusive, and the character of this life is passing. This is a beautiful life, but only in the context of its purpose, which is to prepare us for the next life. Yet we cling to the world—even as it slips through our fingers—only because we have a tough time grasping the reality of Heaven.

This is not to say that the reality of Heaven is something

obvious. When you are eating a sandwich or yelling at the children or mowing the lawn, Heaven is not exactly on your mind. It takes discipline, lots of it, to realize as we operate in this world that there happens to be another, even better one. No matter how much we read the Gospel, pray for light, and keep our hearts centered on God, Heaven seems removed and far away. And that's why death seems so tragic, so terrifying, and so awful. We fear it is absolute.

When death comes to a loved one, we may feel that our faith is at its lowest ebb. The dirt is tossed onto the wooden box and we feel that person is gone forever. We don't see it as the end of something but as the end of everything. Death is not the end of everything. It is simply the end of our soul's relationship with our natural body. When we die, our soul moves to a new place. We experience, for all intents and purposes, a spiritual change of address.

Our Lord spoke to us about the Kingdom and its many mansions, and the idea of geography and residence can help us grasp what death really is. Today our families are on the move constantly, being transferred here and there, leaving communities, neighbors, and dear friends in the wake of their departure. With every move, there is an attendant fear: What will Los Angeles be like? How can I survive without my friend Beth? Will I be happy there? Is this the right thing? Unlike death, a move to another city is our decision. We are given a choice and we decide that the next place will probably be a better one. We are gripped by normal, human apprehension about the unknown, but we don't think for a minute that our life will end just because we're going to a different place. We will still be the same person, with all of our weaknesses and strengths, our talents and our frailties. We will not be changing who we are but where we are. It's our decision and we will make the best of it.

Death is different because it is not our choice, just as it was not our choice to be born. Even if we accept the fact that death is part of our spiritual migration, we'd like to have a say about our departure date. Something makes the unknown that we choose far less frightening than the unknown that someone else chooses for us, even if that Someone is God.

Our incredible lack of trust causes us to accept His Wisdom on issues of this life, but not our eternal life. We trust Him for our daily bread, but not for the Kingdom of Heaven.

The strange thing about our apprehension is that we wouldn't want to live in a material world forever anyway. Sure, this world can be an interesting place, but I don't know anyone who would want to stay here indefinitely, if it meant they'd remain after all of their loved ones had died. We spend billions of dollars every year on hair dyes, face lifts, health clubs, and all the rest, but our efforts to appear young looking don't necessarily reflect an interest in staying here generation after generation. In fact, if I told you, "Great news, pal, you get to live on earth forever," you'd probably celebrate for one night—but then an awful, devastating weariness would come over you. Eventually it would hit you that you'd be out of step with the rest of the world. I don't know one person who could get up every morning, brush his teeth, get dressed, and eat breakfast millennium after millennium. Everyone realizes that this world is a temporary one and that we, as human beings, could not tolerate it as a permanent one. The Christian knows that his soul can live eternally only in Heaven or in hell.

The only way you can enter eternity is to leave this earth. The truth is that death is not the final stop on your journey; eternity is the final stop, and death is how you get there. Your soul is the traveler, and your soul will never die. So why is it so hard to embrace life in the next world?

OUR REAL FEAR OF DEATH: THE UNKNOWN

I often wonder how it must feel to be an infant in the womb, about to be born, moving toward the world of light and sound, knowing nothing, absolutely nothing, of what is to come. The mother knows that the pains of birth are going to be difficult, but she realizes that they are worthwhile. The same comparison can be made between the nonbeliever and the Christian regarding death. The nonbeliever, like the baby, doesn't know that what is to come will be worthwhile. He thinks the pains of death lead to nothing. But the Christian, like the mother, knows that the pains of death lead to everything.

This doesn't make it easy, however. As Saint Monica once said, "I am on my way Home, yet I forget where I am going." For human beings it is impossible to have perfect knowledge of the next world. But unless we have at least a reasonable knowledge of it, we'll always find it difficult to conceive that the process of leaving our bodies is a necessary part of our journey to the Heavenly Father.

I've often heard that it is impossible to dream about your own death. The so-called wisdom behind this myth is that if you dreamed about your death, you'd never wake up. A young Methodist friend of mine did, however, die in his dream, and lived to tell me about it.

Allen had been married just three years, was deeply in love with his wife, and had recently suffered from an almost obsessive fear of what would happen if one of them died. A lot of us put ourselves through these imaginary scenes, wondering, "What if so-and-so died?" and engaging in odd little rehearsals of grief. These rehearsals and fears are absolutely normal and none of us should worry about them.

But Allen's fears were getting a little out of hand, which is why, I suppose, he had this unusual dream. He dreamed that he and his wife were out on the town and were suddenly stopped by a gunman, who wanted their money and jewelry. In a crazed instant, the gunman became impatient and started firing at them. Allen was in terrible fear for his life. But he was even more concerned for the safety of his wife, and as he shielded her, he received several shots in the throat. In minutes, he was "dead."

Allen distinctly remembers the intellectual warmth and serenity of his death in the dream, and then a flood of perfect understanding overwhelmed him. "First I was filled with a perfect forgiveness for the person who killed me. There was no hatred, no fear," he explained. "I was leaving rapidly, and it felt like ages passed as I pulled away from the scene. I saw my wife and had a curious lack of concern, as if I knew that whatever happened to her, she'd be all right. Slowly I felt turned around and tilted upward, and I was filled with perfect assurance and the blissful recognition of God everywhere.''

Thankfully, this dream left Allen with an understanding of eternal life in God's Kingdom. He no longer frets randomly about dying, because he understands that this world is a passage that leads Home. This insight was a special grace for Allen. But there are many assurances in Scripture that we can all turn to in moments of anxiety about our death and our fear of the unknown:

Christ has in fact been raised from the dead, the first-fruits of all who have fallen asleep. Death came through one man and in the same way the resurrection of the dead has come through one Man. Just as all men die in Adam, so all men will be brought to life in Christ. The first man, being from the earth, is earthly by nature; the second Man is from Heaven. As this earthly man was, so are we on earth; and as the Heavenly Man is, so are we in Heaven. And we, who have been modelled on the earthly man, will be modelled on the Heavenly Man (1 Corinthians 15:20–22, 47–49).

Or else, brothers, put it this way: flesh and blood cannot inherit the kingdom of God: and the perishable cannot inherit what lasts forever. I will tell you something that has been secret: that we are not all going to die, but we shall all be changed. This will be instantaneous, in the twinkling of an eye, when the last trumpet sounds. It will sound, and the dead will be raised, imperishable, and we shall be changed as well, because our present perishable nature must put on imperishability and this mortal nature must put on immortality (1 Corinthians 15:50–53).

When this mortal nature has put on immortality, then the words of Scripture will come true: Death is swallowed up in victory. Death, where is your victory? Death, where is your sting? So let us thank God for giving us the victory through our Lord Jesus Christ (1 Corinthians 15:54b–55, 57).

THE SOUL LIVES ON

The most confounding part of all this is simply imagining what is left after our body dies. What is this invisible thing that lives forever called our soul? How can it function without the body?

Many people find it hard to grasp the reality of the soul. But this difficulty has no bearing on whether the soul exists or not. Bishop Sheen once said that the truth is the truth whether everyone believes it or no one believes it. But our incentive to understand is great, for once we comprehend the soul's relationship to the body, we will understand what happens to us when we die.

Most of us make the mistake of picturing the soul as an organ of some kind, like a heart or a kidney or a gaseous form that hovers around the brain. This is a great misconception. If we conceive of the soul as something physically united to the body, then we can't even imagine life after death. The important thing to understand is that the body and the soul are two distinct entities, and that the soul doesn't need the body to exist. The soul is at home in the body, at one with the body, and vivifies the body—but it is not part of the body.

F. J. Sheed compares the soul to a flame and the body to a pot of water. The energies that arise from the flame cause the water to boil and bubble and hiss. The flame animates the pot of water, just as the soul animates the body. Without the flame, the water would just sit there, dormant. The water needs the flame for its life, but the converse is not true. The flame has its own life, just as the soul has its own life, and is dependent only on God for existence.

Our fears about death can be brought under control when we realize that our soul, our true essence, will never die. At some point the pot of water will cease to exist, but the flame will burn on and on toward a perfect knowledge of God's

Goodness. We say we are afraid of dying, but our death has already begun at our birth. We are dying moment by moment, as our soul moves through time in this life to eternity in the next life. Every minute of this life is a step toward eternity. And if it is the eternity of God's Kingdom, it will be bliss of such an extraordinary dimension that no one, not even the angels, could describe it.

THE GRIEF

The truth will set you free, but that doesn't mean that liberation isn't sometimes a painful process. If you are facing the recent or impending loss of someone very dear to you, the reality of Heaven and of that person's eternal soul seems remote and unimportant. The fear and grief you are experiencing center not so much on the nature of death itself, but on your separation and your great loss. As much as I could tell you about the angels and the music and the absolute peace that awaits your loved one in the next life, you only know that you are still in this life and, if you are losing someone, you don't want him to go.

If you are faced with losing someone right now, I know that your existence seems utterly violated and that you feel layers and layers away from the reality that used to be. I know that at this moment you would exchange your own pain, or your loved one's pain, for any other kind of pain. I know the Lord sees and hears your pleas and bargains. "Take me instead." "Let her live and I'll give up everything." "Give him back and I'll do whatever you say." This kind of desperate prayer is normal during times of grief and pain.

Our Lord knows how I mourned and grieved the loss of my mother. Despite all the studying I had done, all the years of prayer I had devoted to God, and all the light God had given me, I still suffered enormous grief at my mother's death. It was a grief that lasted two years and that still pricks me with pain in those odd moments when I see something she liked to eat or when I read one of her favorite Bible passages.

These times, I miss her and am filled with the sorrow of our separation. When she died, I was certain that she deserved to go straight to Heaven and enjoy eternal happiness. But it didn't make me feel any better about losing her.

(People are always surprised to learn that my mother entered our Order late in her life and that I was her Mother Superior. Her twenty years with us in the monastery overcame all the years of bitterness with which she had lived, and made her death a thing of beauty.)

I get a little distressed when I see people at funerals trying to comfort the family and friends of the deceased by pointing out that their loved one is in a "better place." I know they mean well, and most people are at a loss for what to say at a time like this. But that is surely not the point. We all know that the one who died is in a better place (or at least we hope so). We all know that we are going to see them again. We all know that this present life is but a temporary city. We're not dimwits. We're just heartbroken. And to deny our grief at this time—to throw ourselves into an attitude of false acceptance—is not what God asks of us. I'm not putting down people who have a genuine acceptance of their loved one's death. I'm simply cautioning against masking your grief in order to seem like a "better Christian." The fact that you feel grief does not mean that something is wrong with your faith.

Jesus wept when His dear friend Lazarus died, even though He knew He was going to raise Lazarus from the dead. Jesus knows that horrible weight you feel in your heart; He knows that life has been torn apart for you. And when Jesus died, Mary and John and all those who loved Him didn't try to keep a stiff upper lip. What I'm trying to say is that it's okay to cry, to weep, to grieve, and to feel as lost as you do at this moment. Your existence, with the passing of a loved one, has changed. It will never be quite the same, and your grief helps you to adjust your sights on this new reality. You will never feel gladness that your loved ones are deceased. Even though you're glad that they are with God, you will never be indifferent about your loss. The grieving process, if you don't fight it or rush it, will pass. Give yourself time.

But please don't compound your anguish with guilt over the sorrow or weakness you now feel. The fact that you are sorrowful about the loss of a loved one doesn't mean that your faith is weak or that you are ungrateful for the joy your loved one is now experiencing. On a faith level, you know the deceased are better off. That's very important. But it doesn't change the fact that you miss them. I'd be really upset if I thought all my nuns were going to cheerfully accept my death with a rousing "Hosannah, Angelica's finally headed Home!" I hope I never teach them <u>that</u> well. Missing your deceased is a sign of your love, and your love doesn't end just because they died. Love always entails pain because love is sacrificial. Your great continuing love for the person demands that you keep that person's presence in your heart, with memories both beautiful and sad.

THE LONELINESS

I receive so many calls and letters from widows and widowers, and I'm always saddened by the shadowlike existence some of them have created for themselves. If they haven't remarried, they often settle into a state of "half-life," as if their "real life" were a long-running play that is now over and they've been left standing on a darkened stage without a script. They play a "waiting game," waiting idly for their own deaths, their days spent mostly twiddling their thumbs and pacing their empty rooms.

Is it easy to lose the person with whom you have spent so much of your life? Of course not, and I don't mean for a moment to suggest that the burden of loneliness isn't great. It is a tremendous burden, and that is exactly my point. You must view your loneliness as the cross that it is instead of as a misfortune, or a question of circumstance, or a bore.

There is extraordinary sorrow in loneliness, a restlessness that defies description. In loneliness ordinary silence can leave us devastated. The pace of life seems offbeat, slow and awkward. I often imagine what it must have been like for Our

Lord, who left His home in Heaven, sent here by His Father to save a cruel and ill-tempered and ungrateful world. We always picture Him surrounded by the Apostles and His followers, but you and I know loneliness is often most brutal when we are in a crowd. I think of Him walking in His sandals, He Who before knew only Paradise, taking on our human nature while remaining Divine. He spoke with love to everyone, and yet He was misunderstood even by those who loved Him. His loneliness must have been profound in this world of selfish and ignorant human beings.

But He bore His Cross with a dignity that gave His loneliness meaning. Your loneliness can have the same meaning, as powerful and redeeming as the loneliness of Jesus, if only you will offer it to God. Your loneliness can be your sacrifice, not just a period of idleness, not just a time of waiting for your own death. When you deny your loneliness and retreat into a half-life, you waste it. If you have been given the cross to endure the loss of a loved one, you must embrace the pain and emptiness you feel and unite them to the loneliness of Jesus. God needs you to use this time to grow in your own holiness. If you have lost your spouse, remember that you had a different mission before your marriage, and you have a different mission now. Your marriage was a source of happiness for you, but it was not the source of your joy. God was. God is. And God will be forever.

Several years ago, a good friend of mine experienced a great tragedy—the sudden death of her son. Diane's story gives witness to God's tremendous Power and Love in the midst of her heartache.

I was a miserable person. Here I was, twenty-nine years old; I'd had ten pregnancies in ten years and was now the mother of five children. I was very frustrated. I felt penned in, cooped up, trapped. So, I began to search for happiness in the wrong way. . . .

But this particular night as I sat on the beach, I began to weep. My whole life just passed in front of me and I thought, "Dear God, I'm miserable. I don't know what

*I need. I don't know what I'm asking for, but whatever
it takes, please let me begin a new life.''*

*Well, that was seven o'clock on a Tuesday evening.
At seven o'clock the next night, I did begin that new life.
Our eleven-year-old son was killed in a water accident
in front of our home. I was out on the beach that evening
with my husband and I had this frightful feeling that
there was something wrong. I had just told my husband
that I was really afraid and frightened, when I heard a
scream—and I knew that our son Graham had been
killed. It was an instant death. He was in an inner tube
and slammed right into the dock.*

*But I realized at that point I had a choice to make.
That something like this could either destroy me or bring
me to the life I was seeking. And I made the choice to
seek life. I came to realize that there was a God Who
didn't just leave me alone to suffer.*

*I'd heard about Him, way back in school, but I'd never
experienced anything like this—and you never know what
you're going to do when you have something like this to
face. And looking back now, I realize God had prepared
me for that moment.*

Obviously, Diane's struggle did not end there. It took constant prayer and the support of a loving community to sustain
her in this loss. But God has used this tragedy in a most
powerful way. Diane is now co-director of a House of Prayer,
where her love and compassion touch thousands of lives.
God's Power has triumphed over tragedy.

REMEMBERING THE DEPARTED

All of us, at one time or another, will carry the cross of
losing a loved one. In some cases, it will involve the serene
but sad passing of a parent who lived a long and dignified
life. Other times, it will not be part of the normal rhythms of

life, and the suddenness of death, especially the death of a child, may throw us into disorientation, rage, and bitterness.

As Christians, when we must face death, we have two responsibilities. The first is to maintain our relationship with God during these moments, and the second is to truly honor the love we had for the departed by remembering them, praying for them, and seeing them as the gift they truly were and are.

If we fulfill our first responsibility to keep in right relationship with God during these moments of acute pain and suffering, our second responsibility as Christians—which is to honor our departed loved ones—becomes easier. We will be better able to picture the reality of our loved one's continuing existence and joy. That person's joy will be a consolation, even if it doesn't take away the misery we now feel. There are no shortcuts or positive-thinking techniques we can employ when it comes to death. We are going to feel pain and sadness about losing our loved ones, and that's that.

Finally, we must try to remember our departed loved ones by preserving who they were and are, and how they affected our lives in this world as well as how they do now, even in death. I think a lot of us do a disservice to our loved ones by remembering them as perfect individuals: valiant, cheerful, wise, patient, and everything that is good in a person. We start to gloss over the fact that these same folks used to drive us crazy when they would crack their knuckles or interrupt us; in fact, a good 50 percent of the time they were impossible to live with! The head nurse of a local hospital, someone who sees death every day, told me that she overheard a couple talking one evening and was amazed at the wisdom of the dying man's last request: he wanted his wife to remember that he was a pain in the neck!

"If you ever forget how I used to leave pipe tobacco all over the side of my chair, I'll come right back and bop you one," the seventy-year-old cancer patient said to his wife. "And I don't want you to start getting soft on that darn dog Nikki, either. I want you to keep on hating that dog and I want you to remember how I favored him over you nine times out of ten. Sometimes I liked that dog better than you, Margaret, and don't you forget it.''

The man was asking his wife to love him in death just as she had loved him in life, warts and all. He wanted her to preserve his memory, who he was, as rotten as he was—and therefore also as wonderful as he was—instead of recreating some terrible, impersonal, perfect model of a man who had never existed. We tend to sort and file all our memories after we lose a loved one. Instead, we ought to preserve those memories accurately, with the faithfulness and clarity of a historian who knows that it's the truth that keeps us going. Our memories of departed loved ones are all we have. If we substitute sentimental half-truths for the real thing, we'll be left empty-handed. And our grief will be even harder to deal with, because we won't be mourning the loss of our loved one—we'll be mourning the loss of another person, one who never really existed. We won't be able to pick up and go on because nothing could ever compare with the bliss we imagine we experienced while our loved one was still alive.

THE GIFT OF LIFE

A young woman once wrote to us about the death of her father. She had visited him in his hospital room the morning before he was scheduled for major surgery. At first, they spoke to each other about incidentals: the weather, her job, and the fact that her car needed new brake pads.

Finally the father got down to brass tacks.

"You're worried, aren't you, honey?" he said softly.

Lynda started to cry. "I just don't want anything to happen to you, Daddy," she said, holding him close.

Her father's eyes started to well up. He pushed her away for a moment and said, "Sweetheart, did I ever tell you about the stillborn child your grandmother gave birth to, some sixty years ago?" Lynda shook her head.

"It was a baby boy, honey. A big child, who had a hard time finding the light of day. After spanking the boy repeatedly with no response, the midwife gave him up for dead. They wrapped the boy in blankets and placed him on the table.

"Everyone in the family was crying. But your grandmother, in her own inimitable style, was angry. Suddenly, she pulled herself up out of bed, limped over to the table, and picked up her son. She held him by the feet and slapped him over and over, crying, 'Come back, boy! Come back!'

"Within moments there was a whimper. The whimper turned into a howl, and the howl turned into a holler. Some people say I've been hollering ever since," Lynda's father said.

"You . . . you?" Lynda said incredulously. "That was you?"

"It certainly was. And I consider every moment that I've lived on this earth as a gift from God. God gave me the gift of life, and then He gave me the extraordinary grace of knowing just how precious a gift it was. So if it's my time to go, I can't be complaining. As far as I'm concerned, my whole life has been a miracle."

Lynda's father died in the operating room. God called him, and through the grace of God, he was ready. He knew what most of us don't: that none of us will die before God wills it. We must take great consolation in the fact that death comes only with God's permission. Because of His Love, our death could never happen through some arbitrary whim. Even if we meet death through a bizarre accident, we can be sure that God allowed it for the good of our souls. Between our birth and our death, God may pluck us out of danger hundreds, even thousands of times. We'll probably never even know about the most perilous moments in our life.

It takes a lot of trust to know that God, in His perfect Mercy, takes our loved ones at the time that is most favorable for their souls. There are some who are ready to be with God in infancy. Although we cannot know the nature of their mission, we must trust that they have fulfilled it. Others among us need many years to work on our holiness and lots of time to repent. All of us have been given a unique meaning to our existence, and until that meaning is fulfilled, we must continue to wait for God to call us Home.

An Irish priest once shared a comment made by a parishioner in his hometown in County Mayo. It was the evening following the assassination of President Kennedy. The townsfolk had gathered at a neighbor's house and, as was their custom, they talked and visited into the night. " 'Twas an awful thing, Kennedy dying so young, and with so much left to do," the town elder said. A few heads nodded. "A shame it was. I think if he'd lived, he might have saved the world." There was a silence in the room and finally an old woman broke it with her deep brogue, "Ah, but we don't know that, do we? We don't know anything. Only God, in His Wisdom, knows why young Kennedy's left us. Our Jack must have done what God put him here to do."

WHAT DEATH TEACHES US ABOUT THIS WORLD

Some people might think that talking about death is crazy or morose. But I rather like the subject, because it makes people focus on how they are handling life. Discussing death gives us the urgency to explore our relationship with God and to identify the meaning of our lives. If we confront our death as intelligent human beings, we must at the same time confront our own sanctity. Pursuing holiness is not a hobby; it's a full-time job. And thinking about death can help us get our act together.

A Catholic convert I know tells the story of his search for God. Ed was home on leave from the Army, chatting away with his devout Protestant father. They were unpacking his things, and suddenly his father picked up the shiny new dog tags that were lying on the bed.

For a while, the father just stared.

"It says here that you are a Catholic, son," his father finally said. "Are you?"

The young man thought back to that afternoon a few months

before, when he had been asked by the Army information officer to indicate his religion. He was thus forced to consider his own burial and how he wanted to die. He realized at that moment that it was the same way he wanted to live—as a Catholic. He told the officer that he <u>was</u> a Catholic, even though he wasn't.

Ed looked at his father, and his father looked at him. He answered, "Yes, Dad, I guess in my heart I am a Catholic."

"Well, the way I understand it, you either are one or you aren't one," his father said, in his slowest Texas drawl. "It seems to me like you ought to go and talk to a priest."

When we think about our own death, we are forced to consider our own life, both in this world and in the next. We are forced to consider that moment when we will be face to Face with God, when everything we have done or failed to do in this life will be put into sharp focus. I think if we have anything to fear about death, it's that very moment, because while it will surely be sublime, it will also be our day of reckoning. There won't be any more chances to give alms or forgive one more impossible person or go to Confession. Our number will be up. I think I am more afraid of that moment than any in my life, because of what the Lord might show me. In fact, every time I am caught in a web of stress or discouragement, I meditate upon it. It helps me to confront and overcome my own fears.

My meditation begins on my deathbed, which is covered with white linens and a few extra pillows. I say goodbye to all of my beloved nuns and I slip from their arms into the Arms of Jesus. I am speechless. Here is the Son of God. He is like nothing and no one I have ever imagined. After I gather my wits, Jesus gently asks if He could show me something. "Yes, Lord," I whisper in response. "Of course."

I follow Him as we walk a few paces, and then He puts His Arm on my shoulder and turns me around. We are facing the earth, but instead of seeing the classic outlines of the continents, I see billions of faces, filled with peace and serenity and holiness. It is Paradise.

"I just wanted to show you this, Angelica," He says sadly.

"But what is it, Lord? I see that this is earth, but I do not recognize its joy. It is like a dream," I say to Him.

"It is no dream, Angelica. But it was a possibility," He says.

"A real possibility? A world filled with joy? But . . . but how?" I stammer back.

"Angelica," He says, looking into my eyes, "this is what you might have done had you trusted more."

I emerge from my meditation humbled but determined to improve. I am resolved to use more fully the opportunities that the Lord gives me. I reenter my daily life and go back to my writing or to the nuns or to the crew or to the impatient creditor on the telephone. And I ask God in His Mercy to give me just a little more time to try to accomplish His Will.

You and I have an immortal soul. It is permanent, and neither man nor creature can destroy it. The soul can be molded to reflect the Image of God, and its glory in the next life is determined by how well we have followed His Son in this life.

Our present life is precious because it is a school: a school in which to learn how to love God and how to give, choose, and make the right decisions. If we use our time to grow in holiness and to love God with our own unique love, our life will have been well spent. We must realize that our time is short, that this life is but a pilgrimage where we travel from moment to moment until we reach the place He has prepared for us. It is our time to grow.

But when this physical life is over, it's over. I can't tell you the day or the time, but you know that death is coming—for you, for everyone you love, and for everyone you ought to love. Death comes not on our terms, but on God's terms.

Death is our transition from the temporary to the permanent. It is not a certain moment that ends all life for us; it is the beginning of our eternal life. It is what leads us to that awesome moment when we will see the Face of God and take our place in Heaven. Heaven is a reality. It is not some spiritual anesthetic that was concocted to numb the pains of the world. So don't be afraid to die. Pray every day for a good preparation for death. Pray to persevere in a holy and joyful life. Keep before you one very simple goal: that at the moment of your death, you will be able to give yourself totally to God in perfect trust. As a Christian, you are especially blessed because you have already known in this life the saving grace of Our Lord. But you won't know how blessed you actually are until you face that moment of death. Be grateful for your gift of faith.

If you are still panicked by the idea of death, pray to the Father for the grace to understand His gift of eternal life. Your fears of death will begin to slip away. For if you have chosen God in this life, you have already chosen Heaven in the next life. Then death should cause you no terror—for it will be your passage into the Arms of God.

Do not be fearful.
God is with you.

— 11 —

Why Does God Send People to Hell?

SEVERAL YEARS AGO I was in our darkroom developing some negatives for a layout when the Lord decided to clarify the nature of salvation for me. Only God could give a poor nun some badly needed light in her own "dark" room. Anyway, there I stood in the dark, groping around for a couple of duplicate negatives I had just made. I looked everywhere but came up empty-handed.

Finally, I decided to start over. In reaching across the sink to turn on the light, my hand brushed against the counter. There I found the two negatives, which were nearly glued together by the water and the acid. I picked them up and looked at them.

"Angelica, do you see those negatives?" the Lord asked. I nearly jumped to the ceiling. "Yes, Lord," I said.

"Put them together," He said. I obediently put them together and I couldn't see the least bit of difference between the two; it was, in fact, as if they were one. And then the Lord said, "That's Heaven, Angelica. When you see Me face to Face and My Image in you is perfect, you and I will be

One.'' I suddenly, for the first time in my life, could see what perfection might be like.

"Now move the negatives just a little," He said. I took the two negatives and shifted them slightly. The image was blurred, and there was an odd distortion. "That's the image of Purgatory," He said, and I realized that this is what it would be like to see God and yet be imperfect; to long to be with Him, and yet feel stuck, unable to move. Of course: that would be Purgatory.

At last, the Lord said, "Separate them." I felt a chill run down my spine. I separated them and I saw both images stand alone. And I realized what He was saying to me. "Angelica, this is an image of hell. When a soul looks at Me at death and says 'I don't love you' and turns away, it chooses to be in hell. For death is not so much a judgment as a light. It is a time when the soul chooses its final home."

Well, needless to say, I didn't do too much more work in the darkroom that night. I had a lot to think about for days, even weeks, to come. Because for the first time, I fully realized that people aren't sentenced to hell; that in fact, people choose to go there.

Many of our callers ask, "If God is all-forgiving, why does He send people to hell?" It is a favorite question of first-year seminary students. The answer is that God doesn't send people to hell at all. On the contrary, people truly want to go there. "But that's ridiculous, Mother. Why would anyone want to spend eternity burning or tortured with all of those horrible creatures?" The truth, the terrible truth, is that for many people hell is the only possible alternative. You see, salvation, for them, has become repulsive.

WHAT HELL IS NOT

I think we would all agree that hell is an awfully depressing subject, so before we get into the nitty-gritty, let's talk a little bit about salvation. Salvation is serious, but at least it doesn't get us all down in the dumps like the idea of not being saved does. And it's appropriate. Because before we can understand why people actually choose to go to hell, we've got to understand what it is that these people can't stand about Heaven—which, simply put, is God.

Salvation is what life, this life and eternal life, is all about. Now I know we don't think about it every day; in fact, too many of us don't think about it at all because we are so caught up in our backaches and our diets and what we're going to wear tomorrow (not a problem I personally have to deal with). But if we were on really good terms with God and had our own spirituality as our first priority, we'd be thinking about salvation a lot.

How does salvation work? Well, there are two main players who determine your salvation: you and God, and not necessarily in that order. Salvation means "to be saved from" or "delivered from," which gives you a sense of God's more crucial role in the matter. But this does not mean that you are some passive recipient of God's good will and loving nature. On the contrary, you must cooperate with the process, and your cooperation over a lifetime is what makes you either Heaven-bound or a candidate for hell.

Let's do a little "Theology 101" for a refresher. God has revealed to us a few basic points about salvation. At Baptism, we receive the Divine Indwelling of the Trinity—Father, Son, and Holy Spirit. The Father wills that we are saved. The Son merited this salvation for us by shedding His Blood for us. And the Spirit fills our souls with grace so we can achieve the holiness of God.

That is God's magnificent gift to us.

But acceptance of this gift isn't just a matter of saying "Thank you." The faith teaches us that we must want to be saved—and I don't mean a casual "wouldn't that be nice" kind of attitude, I mean really want to be saved, with all our heart and soul. With the honest desire for salvation must come a true sorrow for our sins; again, I mean a true sorrow for our sins, an utterly repentant heart, not merely self-contempt or idle disgust for breaking a few rules here and there. And finally, our salvation is assured by our cooperation with the

Gospel and the teachings of the Church: a willful, intelligent adherence to the Word of God.

So what does this tell us about salvation? It tells us that salvation starts right in the here and now. Salvation began with the Death and Resurrection of Our Lord, but it didn't end with it. Salvation takes place in our souls on a constant, transforming basis, over our whole lifetime. Salvation isn't a ticket to Heaven that you pull out of your pocket and hand to the Lord at your death. It is an accumulation of choices—made for God or against Him.

It is a happy coincidence that in speaking of salvation we get to return to a favorite subject of mine, a subject almost as dear to my heart as humility, which is holiness. I love to spring that on you whenever I can. Because, as you can guess, holiness is your springboard to salvation.

When we talk about your desire to be saved, your repentant heart, and your adherence to God's Word, we've got holiness in a nutshell, because all of it amounts to uniting our own wills to the Will of God. The important thing to remember is that there is one condition, one set of strings, so to speak, that is attached to our salvation. The condition is that we follow God's Will. In Saint Matthew's Gospel, we read "It is not those who say to me, 'Lord, Lord,' who will enter the Kingdom of Heaven, but the person who does the Will of my Father" (Matthew 7:21–22). Now I don't know how you interpret that, but to me, that's a pretty frightening statement. Our Lord is telling us to behave or else! However, it would be wrong to think of Heaven as some kind of club that is nearly impossible to get into, because God wants us to be saved: "It is never the Will of your Father in Heaven that one of these little ones should be lost" (Matthew 18:14).

So we don't need to tiptoe around in fear that every single transgression we make is going to resound to the heavens and damn us forever. You and I have sinful natures and the Lord knows we are going to mess up every now and then. The point is that we must make a constant, vigilant effort to lead good and holy lives.

Last summer a woman came to me and said she was worried about her salvation. Joan had a terrible problem with envy: no matter what she did or how well she held up on the outside, she always found herself battling with petty, envious thoughts, and her envy, mostly, was of other people's holiness. What tricks Satan can play! I told her that she should not give way to anxiety about this weakness, that in her weakness she could glorify God.

"With all due respect," Joan said, "that sounds like a lot of double-talk to me, Mother. I've already got a problem that has me running around in circles. I want to be holy and the reason I'm not is because I envy other people's holiness. Now you're telling me that I can become holy because of the very reason I'm not holy? I'm more confused than ever!"

Apparently, I was not making myself understood. "First of all, you are going to overcome this envy," I said. "You are going to overcome it because you've taken the crucial step of facing it head-on, accepting this self-knowledge, and determining to work on it. That doesn't mean it will ever go away, only that you will conquer it more than it conquers you.

"Second, the reason you are going to conquer this thing is because God is going to help you conquer it. Soon you will honestly marvel at God's Goodness in others. You will look at other people and beam just to know how holy they are and have become, and in doing so, you will reflect not your own goodness, but the Goodness of God. God is at His best in your weaknesses." I also reminded her of something that has been a great comfort to me. "When you find joy in another person's holiness, you get the same merit. Jesus told us that 'Anyone who welcomes a prophet because he is a prophet will have a prophet's reward' (Matthew 10:41). I've always loved that Scripture because you get the reward without the work!" Joan laughed and determined to give it a try.

Sure enough, Joan has undergone a remarkable interior transformation this year, and though she still does battle with envy, her victories have become more numerous, and they all give witness to the Power of God.

The point is that you and I are not going to lose our souls because we have particular weaknesses and frailties. Those weaknesses and frailties are the primary reason we are going to save it. If you have a weakness for lust, lust is your opportunity to glorify God by overcoming it. If you have a weakness for sloth, your industry and concerted efforts to rise above it will be your great test. This is what holiness is all about. This is how you attain holiness in the here and now. No matter how many times you slip and fall, if you are repentant, God will pick you up and help you to try again. And the more you find yourself standing upright, the more natural it will feel to be there.

JUSTICE VERSUS MERCY

As Christians, we talk a lot about the balance between God's Mercy and His justice. And in no area is it more apparent than our pathway to Heaven or hell. I think a lot of people end up choosing hell because they are guilty of the sin of presumption. They feel that they can commit any sin because God is so merciful. They lean on the assumption that they can sin left and right, and that God will bail them out at the last minute.

This is not only a misreading of God's Mercy, but it is also a misunderstanding of how we are saved or not saved.

To begin with, God's Mercy isn't some endless storehouse of good feelings and hugs for "poor, miserable us." True love, and especially Divine Love, doesn't operate on a "gimme" system. God's Mercy is extended to us when we try, fail, repent, and try again; but not when we fail for the fun of it. So don't think for even a second that you are going to lead this worldly, ridiculous life and then on your deathbed say, "I'm sorry," and join the saints in Heaven.

Now you might think that this is amusing, but some people actually "plan" deathbed conversions. "Eat, drink, and be merry," they figure, and foolishly envision a moment when, surrounded by their loved ones, they gallantly apologize for ruining everybody's life and ask God for forgiveness. What they don't know is that when they see God there won't be any way to fake it. They will either truly love God or hate Him. And that's where God's justice comes in.

Granted, there are deathbed conversions and I have witnessed some of the most beautiful ones imaginable. They come when a person is faced with the truth, which at that moment is an astonishment to them, and because there is true goodness in their hearts. Because they have not shut God out completely, they are in awe and truly repentant of their sins. They long for God, they long to be saved, and God in His Mercy facilitates their salvation.

But justice must also come with this mercy. Imagine the worst kind of character, a pornographer or a drug dealer, a person who indulged in every kind of sin with a vengeance, a person who with utter hatred in his heart hurts everyone around him, who caused the deaths of others and lured countless innocent people into sin and corruption. This person on his deathbed is still laughing and mocking all of the "weak and fainthearted" who spent holy, disciplined lives, trying their best to please God. He jeers at everyone who tried to love him, who tried to share Jesus with him, who tried time after time to show him the light.

Now it would be terribly unjust, not to mention impossible, to have an unrepentant sinner live in Heaven with Mary, Saint Paul, Saint Peter, and all the Apostles and saints. Heaven would not be Heaven if he were part of it. But God's Justice is extraordinarily loving and kind. The process of salvation provides that this man—and all men—can choose for themselves, every moment of their lives and at the special moment of death, just where they want to spend their eternity.

THE ROAD TO HELL

Our eternal life, then, is affected deeply by our own behavior. The person who turns away from God must do it deliberately. This is why what I call "lukewarmness" is such a danger. It's not all that hard to follow the rules and to be a good citizen and a nice person. But if that's all you think is required of you, you're sadly mistaken. If you—with the light that has been given you—shirk true holiness, then you could be paving your own road to hell. God doesn't grade on the curve. It's not a matter of your being in the sixtieth percentile of "good people." You have a unique opportunity for holiness, and what you make of that opportunity determines how you will be judged.

This is the great problem with tepidity. When you are indifferent, when you procrastinate, when you put off loving God and giving to God in the present moment, you are, so to speak, playing with fire. It is far easier to develop a hardness of heart toward God than to serve Him well. Selfishness is one of those things that can set in quickly, and before you know it, you can waste all the spiritual gains you have made in this life.

The person who chooses hell starts making that choice on earth. When there is a choice to be made between his will and the Will of God, he chooses against God. At first, he feels uneasy. Then the uneasiness grows into resentment and God, in his mind, becomes some sort of nag. He starts to deny that his sins are sins, and his contempt for God builds; indeed, in his denial of his sins, he is "calling God a liar" (1 John 1:10). Soon, God becomes a threat to that person's "way of life." An enemy. A competitor. An intolerable interference. When a person is in this state he runs a great risk, for if death should come to him, he will likely choose against God. This shouldn't be such a surprise. If a person starts to love sin, if he loves to lie, commit adultery, cheat, or kill, his ability to love has turned toward himself and away from God. He will not tolerate anyone who accomplishes God's Will because it interferes with his own. And that person's will, in this awful condition, may become fixed.

For most of us it is hard to imagine this state of soul, but that doesn't mean we should all breathe a sigh of relief. I cannot say what it would take for your soul or my soul to be led away from God. Temptation can come in forms that are not obvious or easily discernible. Our own capacity for self-deception makes a cocky attitude decidedly inappropriate. As Saint Peter put it, "Be calm but vigilant, because your enemy the devil is prowling round like a roaring lion, looking for someone to eat" (1 Peter 5:8). So when you are pushed or strained or sorely tempted to sin, remember with humility that you are capable of "blowing it" and turning your back on God.

THE CHOICE

At death, all of us receive full light. If there is one guarantee in this life, it is that all of us will see the Face of God. I will. You will. Your mean old neighbor will. Your father will. Your little girl will. So will all our friends and relatives, even people who seem to us to be hardhearted or cynical or simply unmoved by religion. We should all understand the truth, which is that all of us will see God face to Face at death. The question is whether or not we die in the state of grace. Indeed, if we have grace in our souls at death, we will recognize God's great Love for us, we will tremble at His Power, and we will realize how unlike Him we have been.

More than any other single factor, God requires repentance to enter the kingdom. He can't forgive a sinner unless the sinner acknowledges his sin. If an impasse is reached, if a devastating contest of wills takes place at the moment of death—then, upon seeing God, the sinner will simply turn his face away. An eternal rejection of God is made at that moment and lasts forever. The suffering that this person has chosen is indescribable and immeasurable.

It is hard to know why some of us end up making this choice. A person in this state is so steeped in his own pride, so devoted to his own will, that he cannot accept anything that contradicts it. He does not choose suffering as much as he rejects a love he has found impossible to accept. His suffering in hell for all eternity is simply the result.

But what is hell like? No one has actually gone to hell and come back to talk about it, of course. We do have some bits and pieces from Scripture that shed light, as it were, on the darkness. Saint Matthew's Gospel says to those who refuse to serve, "Go away from Me, with your curse upon you, to the eternal fire prepared for the devil and his angels" (Matthew 25:41). Here we see hell as separation, and later in the same chapter we see that hell is also punishment: "And they will go away to eternal punishment, and the virtuous to eternal life" (Matthew 25:46). However, the most painful parts of hell are the despair, hopelessness, and eternal hatred. Just as each soul's place in Heaven will vary, I think that each soul's particular torments in hell will be unique, according to the kind of sins the soul was guilty of in this life. But whatever the agony, it will be uninterrupted, pure, relentless, and unending. The possibility of hope will be over.

In 1917, three children were given a vision of hell. Francisco, Jacinta, and Lucia saw the Apparitions of the Blessed Virgin Mary at Fatima, Portugal, and as Sister Lucia recorded in her *Memoirs,*

> *Our Lady showed us a great sea of fire which seemed to be under the earth. Plunged into this fire were demons and souls in human form, like transparent burning embers, all blackened or burnished bronze, floating about in the conflagration, now raised into the air by the flames that issued from within themselves together with great clouds of smoke, now falling back on every side like sparks in a huge fire, without weight or equilibrium, and amid shrieks and groans of pain and despair, which horrified us and made us tremble with fear. The demons could be distinguished by their terrifying and repellent likeness to frightful and unknown animals, all black and transparent. This vision lasted but an instant. How can we ever be grateful enough to our kind heavenly Mother, who had already prepared us by promising, in the first Apparition, to take us to Heaven. Otherwise, I think we would have died of fear and terror.*

To alleviate the horror and fear that resulted from this terrible vision, the children often recited a short prayer taught to them by Our Lady of Fatima:

*O my Jesus! Forgive us our sins; save us from the
fires of hell. Lead all souls to Heaven, especially those
in most need of Thy Mercy.*

Little Jacinta prayed for long periods of time on her knees,
saying this prayer over and over again "to save souls from
hell! So many go there! So many!" She wished that she could
show hell to all people, so that they would sin no more and
thus avoid the eternal fire. Although she was only a young
child, she zealously embraced penance and mortification after
this vision, so great was her desire to prevent any more souls
from going to hell.*

THE CONSEQUENCES OF EVIL

There are many in today's world who deny the existence
of Satan and hell. In *The Screwtape Letters*, C. S. Lewis
wrote that the devil's most cunning trick is to persuade us
that he does not exist. To dread hell, to tremble at its thought,
is to have reached a great spiritual milestone. A lot of people
shrug off the idea of hell in the same way that they shrug off
the idea of the devil, as if it were all just a scare tactic invented by some bored theologians. And yet why should we
take so lightly a place and a person whom God takes so seriously?

Hell is the absence of God. It is impossible for us to imagine, and so we must rely on vivid imagery of fire and torture
to help us comprehend the kind of suffering a life without
God would entail. But our imaginations are insufficient. We
cannot picture a universe robbed of all goodness and hope.
We cannot grasp a state of utter and complete despair.

And yet there are those among us who do choose it. Our
choice of hell begins in this life, as we opt for our own will,
for kicks, for sin, and for selfish indulgences. God gave us

---

*Fr. Louis Kondor, S.V.D., ed., *Fatima in Lucia's Own Words* (Fatima, Portugal, Postulation Centre, 1976), pp. 108–110.

free will and we exercise it. We make our sinful choices like there was no tomorrow. But there is a tomorrow. And while we can make any choice we like, we can never dictate what the consequences of that choice will be. The consequences of sin are simply part of the package, and they are devastating.

When we take our puny wills and hold them up against the Will of God, against the Will of the One Who wills our existence, we prove ourselves to be mere fools. Our sinfulness is a matter of buffoonery. Idiocy. And sadness for all whom we hurt in the process. But at death, our bad choices can become a permanent tragedy. For the sins we have chosen have a horrible consequence: the hatred of God. In the end, the price we will pay is eternal damnation.

This is why you and I must keep our eyes looking upward, Heavenward, and why we must tend to that particular mission of holiness that is our own. Our love, which is expressed by our holiness, must be a shining example of God's Love for us. That example will then encourage others to choose God. As long as people choose hell, there is much work to be done.

Choose God.
He has already chosen you.

— 12 —

What Will Heaven Be Like?

M Y GRANDFATHER WAS a robust, lovable character, the kind of man who was larger than life even in life. He had a great devotion to the Blessed Virgin Mary, and every time someone would mention her name, he would tip his hat or salute. The whole family loved Grandfather, and so we were saddened by the fact of his dying.

But not by his death.

Grandfather's last days were spent paralyzed, lying in bed. For months, he had not been able to move. One morning my mother went in to change the linens on his bed. As she started to slide the pillow gently from underneath his head, she realized that someone was at the door. She gasped as she saw two figures standing there. The two men were old friends of my grandfather's, but they had been dead for more than a decade.

The taller of the two gentlemen called out to my grandfather. "Anthony," he said. To my mother's astonishment, my grandfather slowly sat up in his bed. He opened his eyes and strained to see his friends from years past and, as he recognized them, two tears rolled down his cheeks. "No," he said weakly, shaking his head. "No."

The man called out again. "Anthony," he said. And again, "Anthony." My grandfather sat up once more. Suddenly, his face lit up with an extraordinary peace. He smiled from ear to ear, and he said to his old friend, "Yes."

Grandfather lay back in bed and closed his eyes. Within moments, he was dead.

Of one thing I am sure: Anthony Francis is in Heaven. Now I know that a lot of people think that Heaven is a kind of vast celestial landscape which is thinly populated by the saints, the angels, and only a handful of others who really paid their dues to get there. But I consider it much more plausible that millions and millions of souls rest in Heaven—the unborn children, the suffering who were united to the Will of God at death as well as in this life, and the faithful who were ready to see God's Face in Heaven because it was the Face they so nearly resembled on earth. Many of my Catholic friends aim for Purgatory, thinking Heaven is beyond their grasp. Well, I don't buy that attitude for a minute. I think all of us have the opportunity to go to Heaven, like my grandfather—to join not only the angels and the saints, but also our family and friends in a land of incalculable bliss.

"But what is Heaven, Mother?" you ask. "Is it nonstop harp music and fluffy clouds? Is it a place somewhere up in the sky? Is it in my heart? Why should I spend my whole life trying to get there?" These are excellent questions and I will answer every one of them, because I want to convince you that Heaven is not a boring concept that was invented to make you feel better about dying. Nor is it some endless vaporlike existence where you sit around idly waiting for something to do.

Granted, Heaven is a difficult subject to discuss; after all, we're talking about the residence of the Creator of the universe. But difficult or not, the reality of Heaven is within our intellectual grasp if we turn an eager mind to Scripture and to the teachings of the Catholic faith. Those of you who think that Heaven is a tedious subject have a big surprise coming, because the truth about Heaven could—and should—change every minute of the life you now lead.

Our place in Heaven depends on our day-to-day behavior and attitudes. I, for one, have a big fear that when I finally make it to Heaven, Saint Peter and Saint Paul are going to give me the cold shoulder because of all the wisecracks I've made about them. But on a much deeper level, we Christians must confront the hard truth that our holiness isn't just a hobby or some weak-kneed effort to "be good." Our holiness is the serious business of personal salvation. It is the business of accepting that Jesus died and rose from the dead for our sins, to obtain for us our salvation and the riches of Heaven. And the more we learn about Heaven, the more we realize that Heaven is what our stay on earth is all about.

OKAY, THEN, WHAT IS HEAVEN?

I think that most of us, if pressed about the location of Heaven, would answer that it is somewhere "up there." We look to a God in the clouds when we want to praise Him or thank Him or ask Him for His Grace. When someone mentions a deceased friend or relative, we raise our eyes and murmur, "May he rest in peace." Believer and nonbeliever alike suppose that there is a spiritual law of gravity which says that things unencumbered by a body must necessarily float upward, Godward, to Heaven. I know I can't help but think of Heaven when I look out the window of a plane on a beautiful, sunlit day when mounds and mounds of clouds strike a perfect formation against the blue sky. And Saint John talks about the ups and downs of Heaven and earth in his Gospel when he says, "No one has gone up to Heaven except the One Who came down from Heaven, the Son of Man Who is in Heaven" (John 3:13).

All of this suggests that Heaven is a place, and it is.

But Heaven is also a state. Jesus tells us that the Kingdom of Heaven is within us because the Father, Son, and Holy Spirit dwell in us: "If anyone loves Me he will keep My

Word, and My Father will love him, and We shall come to him and make Our home with him" (John 14:23). Later, Saint John also tells us, "God is love and anyone who lives in love lives in God, and God lives in him" (1 John 4:16).

So to begin with, it is important to realize that Heaven is both a place and a state. If we are with God, and God is in us, then we have Heaven on earth, and the business of Heaven on earth is called holiness. The people we know who radiate joy in this life are obvious. One need only look into the eyes of Mother Teresa, or the father of a child being christened, or an elderly person facing her death without fear to see the true joy of a Christian who carries Heaven in his heart. The first Christians were exemplary models of joy: they sang as the lions were unleashed upon them in the arenas of hatred; they praised God as they were crucified, stoned, and persecuted. Saint Peter rejoiced that he was found worthy to be crucified upside down. Saint Stephen's face glowed like the face of an angel as he was stoned to death.

These Christians had Heaven in their hearts and, if their joy seems remote to us, it is a distance of our own making. Still, this "Heaven on earth" is the Heaven most of us can grasp; we can take intellectual shelter in the false notion that Heaven is actually a symbol rather than a reality, or that Christian joy is some kind of psychological condition or "inner peace" rather than the hard-fought perfection of the soul. Somehow, this notion of Heaven seems palatable to our material sensibilities.

But the Heaven of the next life can't be set aside, reinterpreted, or dismissed as easily. Here we are talking about another world, a world we cannot see or hear or imagine. This Heaven is the perpetual vision of God. Saint Augustine said that "Faith is to believe what we do not see; the reward of faith is to see what we believe." When we die, the souls who resembled God, sought God, and were occupied with God are granted the Beatific Vision, the awesome experience of being "face to Face with God." This is the Heaven of eternal life and the key to the mysteries of our faith. It is this Heaven that most of us have a hard time understanding.

Now I know that if your arthritis is killing you and the kids are driving you up the wall, none of this seems to matter much right now. "I've got eggs to fry, Mother. Talk to me when I'm on my deathbed." This is where we miss the whole point of Christianity. Every moment that we are cavalier about our destiny in the next life is a wasted moment of this life. As Christians, our lives in this world only have meaning because they determine the nature and quality of our eternal life. Our lives do not have meaning because we are plumbers or presidents or polo players. They do not even have meaning because we are nice or good or generous. No, they have meaning only because life is given to us by God—and for <u>His</u> Purpose, which is for us to reach the heights of Heaven. But we must remember that Heaven isn't just some pastel place that we dwell in after death. Heaven is the fruit of a lifetime of struggle. And the pursuit of Heaven begins here on earth with what Christians call holiness.

HEAVEN CAN'T WAIT

Most of us have this crazy notion that when we die we will suddenly be confronted with three big doors that lead to Heaven, hell, or Purgatory, as if eternity were some kind of daytime quiz show. While we feel that a future in Heaven would be nice, most of us figure that it is beyond our reach. Our hopes are pinned on "Door Number 2," the door to Purgatory, and we hope against hope that when the time comes we'll be able to slide into the back of that "great halfway house in the sky." Now this is no slight on the "halfway house"—Saint Thomas assures us that the saddest day in Purgatory is a thousand times more joyful than the happiest day on earth—but the truth is that you don't slide into any dimension of your spiritual life.

All of us begin our journey to Heaven, hell, or Purgatory right here on earth. Our supernatural life is the journey of our soul, and like any journey, the first steps are just as important as the last steps and all the steps in between. So if you're thinking that you can slide into Purgatory at the last minute, or that you might be able to talk your way into Heaven after a life of disgraceful behavior, or if you're one of those "just-in-case Christians" who figure you'll get holy in your old age, forget it. Your eternal life is on God's time, not your time, and the time to start working on it is now.

What we must realize is that our soul grows and matures and achieves its ultimate level of holiness in this life and this life only. I know so many who are members of the "now" generation, and it seems like the only thing they put off until "later" is the development of their spiritual life. But "later" could mean "never" in the context of the supernatural. All the elements of this life—the sorrows, the joys, the setbacks, the trials—combine with the grace of God to mold and form us into His Image. Every piece of truth that we accept, every opportunity for holiness that is placed in our path, every slap in the face that we must accept as Jesus accepted it pulls us closer to Jesus or propels us away from Him. Whatever capacity for love the soul has grown to at death will determine its glory and joy in Heaven.

And yet, some of us have a hard time focusing on this faraway place. It is as if our eyes are covered by a strange haze that keeps us from grasping the reality of our true purpose in life. Sometimes the haze is sheer intellectual laziness. Other times it is sin, riches, lust, alcohol, pride, desire for human glory. If you find it difficult to focus on Heaven as the purpose of your life, take a look at what it is—or who it is—that is keeping you away from it. What is it that makes you desire to live in a mud shack rather than a mansion? What is it in your life that clouds your vision so badly?

HAPPINESS IS NOT JOY

I have concluded that the pursuit of "happiness" keeps more people out of Heaven than there are angels to count them. "Happiness, Mother?" Yes, happiness. As Christians, we have failed to make a crucial distinction between the pursuit of happiness and the pursuit of joy. I hope when I get to the Kingdom I'll be able to have a long talk on this subject with the Founding Fathers of our country, because when they threw "happiness" into the "life and liberty" equation, they granted it a stature it truly does not deserve.

You see, happiness is a happening, and because it is a happening, it's bound to change or disappear or simply die. Happiness disappoints us because it depends on other people, other places, other things. Your husband comes home from a lousy day at work and he's miserable, while little Junior, who got an *A* in science, is on cloud nine. The next day, your husband gets a raise and your son gets an *F*—and the two have traded places before your very eyes. Happiness is not exactly what I'd call reliable. When you get hung up on its pursuit, your attitude shifts from a reliance on God and on your spiritual life to a reliance on whatever external factors give you pleasure. You fight and claw to control the uncontrollable, to win that which cannot be won, and the great casualty of this obsession with happiness is your holiness.

Now don't get me wrong—I'm not saying that all of us should go around with frowns on our faces. When I hear my nuns laughing it is, to me, like a choir of angels. But if my well-being depended on their laughter or their love, I'd be in a pickle. You and I have got to face facts: there is sadness in this life. There is suffering all around us. It would be folly to devote an entire lifetime to our own passing comforts or to the "good times."

The attitude that says, "All I want in life is to be happy" has diverted millions of souls from achieving knowledge of God, the true source of everlasting happiness. And this is why, as Christians, we must distinguish between the pursuit of happiness and the pursuit of joy. Joy in our hearts is the awakening of God in our souls, Whose Kingdom we can know and experience here on earth. Joy is the knowledge that God's Will is being accomplished in our lives. It is this knowledge that gives us the strength to dance for joy when we are persecuted, to endure insult and injury with the peace of Jesus, to take whatever comes—the good, the bad, and all the rest—as the Will of God. Joy is what comes from the Divine Indwelling of the Father, Son, and Holy Spirit in our souls.

I remember a recent episode in the history of our network, when we were trying to acquire air time on one of the major satellites. We were faced with the possibility of losing the network if the negotiations proved unsuccessful. It was a terrifying proposition—to think that five years of ministry could end in a moment because of an inability to reach the people. And there was added frustration in having to deal with people whose information changed from one day to the next.

I've always known that it was hard to be a Christian in the business world. But it was all I could do to call upon my forty-two years of religious life to help me realize that God would bring good out of this mess. I had to remember that the network was God's in the first place, and my prayer had to be one of abandonment. If God wanted the network to end after five years, I had to be content with that. I wouldn't like it, but the abandonment to His Will brought me a sense of joy in the midst of all the turmoil.

With God's Grace, we can achieve Heaven in our lives on earth by following the basic teachings of Jesus, those teachings that are profoundly simple, and yet so often elusive.

- We can be faithful to the duties of our state in life, whether we are single, married, or have a religious vocation, as we obey God's Commandments.
- We can respond to the daily crises of life with the gentleness, courage, and dignity of Our Lord.
- We can make God the center of our lives, always making more room for Him in our hearts.
- We can trust God, no matter how ridiculous, perilous, or mysterious our plight may be; we can trust that He is watching, guiding, and protecting us even when all looks so horribly lost.

The pursuit of joy in this life is not as difficult as it seems. It is not reserved for the cloistered nun or the inspired preacher or the tireless charity worker. Joy, an uncanny joy, a joy that allows you to take the most bitter experiences in life and get through them with the peace of God, is for you. It all boils down to three words: accepting God's Will. We know that this is sometimes easier said than done, but with Faith, Hope, and Love as your spiritual companions, you will grow in this direction. The joy you can achieve by uniting your tremendous desire, energy, and will to the Will of God is liberating beyond your wildest dreams. When you accept God's Will in every aspect of your life you will find God providing you with strength, courage, and a dignity that resounds to the heavens. It resounds to the heavens because it doesn't have far to go. Heaven, you see, is suddenly in your heart.

HEAVEN, THE PLACE

Now I know that some people think it's downright audacious to talk about the "other" Heaven—after all, only Our Lord has made the journey from Heaven to earth and then back again—but I see no point in retreating from the subject, especially since it is discussed with such frequency in Scripture. This does not please everyone. I remember receiving a call from an irate woman during a seven-part series I was giving on Heaven.

"Mother!" she screamed into the telephone. "Haven't you ever read the Bible? Don't you know that Saint Paul himself says 'No eye has seen and no ear has heard'* what God has prepared for us in His Kingdom? Where do you get off talking about a place you've never seen?"

"That's exactly my point," I said. "Nothing I say can even come close to what Heaven is really like. Doesn't your preacher ever talk about hell?"

"Well, of course," she said hotly.

"Has he ever been there?" I asked again.

"Certainly not!" she said.

"Well, if your preacher can talk about hell without ever having made a round trip, then why shouldn't I talk just a little bit about Heaven?" I replied. "It is, after all, the goal of our eternal lives as Christians!" She reluctantly agreed.

---

*1 Corinthians 2:9.

My point is that I am not afraid to talk about Heaven. On the contrary, I'm afraid not to talk about Heaven. I worry when Christians shy away from subjects just because they are too difficult or because they strain the brain too much. We can't know everything there is to know about Heaven: Our Lord makes it clear that we are not capable of fathoming the full knowledge of Heaven. But we do have a few important revelations of what is to come, especially as affecting the way we live our day-to-day lives.

For one thing, we know that in Heaven—just as on earth—everyone is different. Just as our talents, our beauty, our intellects, and our temperaments vary here on earth, so our positions and personalities in Heaven will also vary. This makes sense because everyone relates to God in a different way. All my nuns are completely different. We've got short ones, tall ones, funny ones, pensive ones, lighthearted ones, and melancholic ones. We don't pray alike. We don't look alike. We don't like the same food or songs or jokes. But when you look into the eyes of each of my nuns you see God. Their beauty is in their unique love for the Lord, and in Heaven their uniqueness will be valued and preserved.

But there's even more. For in Heaven we will see how, in God's Plan, perfect justice prevails. We will see that those who suffered pain or humiliation on earth are—because of their suffering—rewarded. We will marvel as the poor, the maimed, and the persecuted of this world, as well as those who with a humble heart tried to be holy, take their place among the saints.

My heart goes out to parents who lose children through miscarriage. A child conceived in love in whom God breathed a soul is suddenly rushed into eternity. But in the midst of pain, heartache, and a sense of loss, parents can take heart. The first voice their child ever heard was the Voice of God. It never heard anyone speak in anger, jealousy, or contempt. And while we feel sadness that the child never saw a flower or a tree or the face of its parents, we must remember that the first thing that child did see was the Face of God. In the short term, it was terribly deprived. But in eternity, it lives in extraordinary bliss.

Saint Peter tells us: "If you can have some share in the sufferings of Christ, be glad, because you will enjoy a much greater gladness when His Glory is revealed" (1 Peter 4:13). Joy in Heaven will not be equal for all of us. We will each be rewarded to the extent that we have responded to our sufferings in this life with the love and dignity of Jesus. The rewards of Heaven will more than counterbalance the pain and trials of this world. But that is just one aspect of the justice that will manifest itself in our eternal life. For ultimately, it is the manner in which we cooperate with God in our lives—during bad times and good times—that determines our place in Heaven. The road to Heaven is paved by laughter and by tears, all aligned to the Will of God in the present moment. The Christian who accepts his lot cheerfully and who knows that in the grand scheme of life all things must pass will lead the procession to Heaven's gate.

A lot of people ask me about the billions of souls who are not Christians, those who never got a chance to know Jesus Christ. "Will God bar these people from Heaven?" they wonder. The answer is no. God will judge us according to the light we have received on earth and how we have lived by that light. By "light" I mean our degree of knowledge of God. Someone who has not had the opportunity to hear about God will not have the same degree of knowledge as one who has been exposed to the love of Jesus.

Our place in Heaven is determined by what we did with all the gifts and trials we received in this life. Those who were baptized and educated as Christians have a higher obligation to holiness than those who were not. But each person will be measured individually: those graced with deep knowledge and insight and gifts will be graded with a much stricter pen, and those who simply held true to the God-infused distinctions of right and wrong will be more gently judged. But concern yourself first and foremost with your own salvation. If tonight you were called by God, would you make it past Saint Peter's gate?

WHAT WILL I DO IN HEAVEN?

There is something in our nature that causes us to think that Heaven, even in all its glory, might be kind of dull. The idea of spending our eternal lives praising God sounds, quite frankly, a little repetitive. Sure, we love our Father in Heaven, but we are used to the rewards of everyday life: a spontaneous hug from a child, a retreat to a desolate beach, a steaming plate of spaghetti. Our finite minds cannot fathom how the joys of Heaven might ever exceed the highest moments of happiness we have experienced here on earth. Further, eternity sounds like a long, long time. And because we measure everything in terms of this world, we see eternity as endless minutes, hours, and days instead of a place where there is no time at all. Eternity seems like it might just be too long.

Well, I can tell you that if it were possible to be embarrassed in Heaven, we'd see a lot of red faces, because this fear that the Kingdom will be boring is utter nonsense. And the problem with this kind of thinking, especially if we cling to it, is that it stunts our spiritual growth. We get locked into thinking that Christianity is a tidy system of rules, and we miss the depth of spirituality that it entails.

The promise of God's Kingdom takes time and prayer to grasp fully, and if you are just setting sail on your spiritual journey, I wouldn't try to take it all in at once. But do get it out of your head that Heaven might be boring. Think of it from this standpoint: everything you love about your life on earth has been a gift from God. Every grain of it is of His Own making, including the making of you! Now if He gave you this life as a testing ground, and clearly stated that Heaven was the reward of this testing ground, why would you doubt the reward? Why would God devise an eternal system that, in the end, would only bore you? Don't you think He has better things to do?

Alas, we seem so uncertain of His Greatness, even as we stare it in the face. We doubt that Heaven will be "fun," and we worry that it might not even exist at all. Well, let's erase all the fine robes and harps and jewels out of your imagination and give you, instead, a picture you can comprehend. Push aside those fluffy clouds, and imagine how you might think and feel in a state of utter bliss—for that is what Heaven is all about.

- We will learn why God permitted the trials and illnesses and heartaches of this life.
- We will see the Justice and Mercy of God, as the disadvantages of this life are rewarded by high stations in Heaven.
- We will see all our faults and weaknesses fall away from our souls like scales from a fish.
- We will understand the mysteries of nature and the universe.
- We will be able to comprehend great truths with ease. Nothing will be difficult.
- We will see the mysteries of God as they continue to unfold.
- We will love and be loved by everyone, and never have any aversion or antipathy toward anyone.
- We will always have something new to do and learn in Heaven, something different to be joyful about.
- We will never feel worthless, lonely, slighted, discouraged, depressed, or stupid.
- We will never feel anger, resentment, hatred, jealousy, or ambition.
- We will never experience hunger, thirst, or poverty.
- We will never again be afraid.

How could you ever think of giving all this up in exchange for a life of sin? It would be like trading a chest full of diamonds for a tray of coal.

In Heaven we will, for the first time, encounter full knowledge of ourselves and of our lives, and we will not be afraid of the truth we discover. Pope John XXIII had a little sign on his desk that simply read: "Know yourself." Self-knowledge is critical to the spiritual life, but so often we run from the hard truths about our sinfulness and our weaknesses. In

Heaven, we will get the whole picture, but we won't run and hide in shame. We will see all of those gifts and talents that are ours and ours alone, and we will direct them to the praise and glory of God's Name. We will have so much light that we will be free to love ourselves and every other person in God's Creation—not because we are so good, but because God is so good.

Self-knowledge will fascinate us. But our intellects will not stop growing with that, because in Heaven all the great mysteries will be explained. I can't wait to sit down and talk to Saint Thomas Aquinas and Saint Augustine about the Trinity and all the other "biggies" that have puzzled me. When I was growing up, I was the kind of student who had to work hard for my F's; I just didn't have time for books and homework and the other staples of childhood. The very idea that I might be able to stroll down the corridors of Heaven and discuss without trepidation the great truths of our spiritual existence simply boggles my mind.

Not only will our intellects take flight in Heaven, but our memories and wills will be perfectly united to the Will of God. We won't even be a fraction of an inch apart from what He wants for us, for we will be without sin. Can you imagine a "perfected you"? No sin exists—or could exist—in Heaven. Although you will help God in His battle against evil, everyone around you and everything within you will be pure. There will be no hatred, no jealousy, no lust, no sloth—and no pride. You and I will have no evil inclinations or weaknesses. We will never vacillate from the Will of God. We won't be tempted or tested ever again. Nor will we be tormented any longer by the memory of our sins. Our memories will be totally free of anger, fear, guilt, hurt, regret, and resentment. In their place will be love, compassion, and mercy. All our frailties will have melted away and we will be who we always longed to be. Sometimes I like to meditate upon an Angelica who doesn't yell at people, an Angelica who is patient and relaxed. I think of what it would be like to wake up with gentleness each morning, instead of greeting each day like a fire drill.

Endless joy, I promise you, won't be boring, for in Heaven

you will never be idle. In fact, you'll probably spend your eternal life working. But don't jump to conclusions. You won't be doing the kind of work you have done here on earth. You won't be washing dishes or laying bricks or writing memos in Heaven. The only reason you did all these things on earth was to feed your family and to pay your rent. But in Heaven there are no mouths to feed or mortgages to pay. What you will do is pray for those you love on earth and, through prayer, guide and even inspire them. You will help to shape souls and touch hearts. Your talents—all of them— will still be yours, and God will take those qualities, your wit, your logic, your patience, and your love, and use them all for His Honor and Glory.

KEEPING OUR SIGHTS ON HEAVEN

No doubt about it, it's hard work trying to imagine Heaven, and whatever we come up with is guaranteed to fall short. But that's okay. What is not okay is that our inability to imagine it all, the fact that we don't have a four-color travel brochure and a map to get there, stops us from believing that it's real. We are "realists," or so we say, and yet the confines of our realities make for a pretty poor truth. We live in the shoe box of our senses, and our limitations prevent us from gazing at the spiritual realities of God's world. When people talk to us about things we cannot see or places we cannot visit, we get nervous.

But this doesn't mean we should give up—to do so would be to give up on the truth—nor does it mean that we should become obsessed with its understanding. You and I will enter the Kingdom of Heaven if we carry in our hearts a simple love for God. God is not asking that we memorize the works of Saint Thomas Aquinas or Saint Augustine. He's not asking that we comprehend all the mysteries. He only asks that we regard the kingdom of this world, as crummy as it is, with love and patience—and that we desire the Kingdom of Heaven, as wonderful and as mysterious as it is, with Faith, Hope, and Love.

If we relegate Heaven to the status of "door prize" or a shallow motivation to "be good" or the pot at the end of the rainbow, we'll never make it. If we think that our faith will win us favors or stop our suffering or make us rich, we're sure to be disappointed. When we reflect back on the early Christians and martyrs, those simple, quiet souls who loved God through the best of times and the worst of times, then we know that we have much preparation to do before we can join these people in the Kingdom. Then we will stop our petty complaining. Then we will set our sights on the place we cannot see.

So when you ask me, "What will Heaven be like?" I must answer that it will be more perfect than any of us could say. Whatever your best concept of total happiness is, it's nothing compared to Heaven.

In Heaven, you will never feel the absence of anybody or anything. We've probably all met someone who was very attached to a pet. I remember meeting an elderly woman who spent great sums of money on her Chihuahua "Pepe," and had even purchased a burial plot for him in a pet cemetery. She came to me one day very distressed over the fact that she wouldn't see Pepe in Heaven.

"How can I possibly be joyful in Heaven without my dear Pepe?" she asked. I tried to maintain my composure and be sensitive to her inordinate attachment. I explained that in this life God provides various comforts for us, often to alleviate our loneliness, and in the case of pets, to allow us the opportunity to enjoy companionship. However, in Heaven we won't need the things that are so necessary in this life. When we die, we will bring only ourselves, our souls, and our love. We will stand alone before God. At that moment, God will become our "all." We will have no need for pets or any worldly comforts, for there will be no voids, no needs. Our attachment will be to God alone. Once God becomes our "all," we will have everlasting and sublime joy. We will be totally content. And we will lack for nothing.

As we move forward on our spiritual journey, we realize

that Heaven is not an invention of the mind: it is the goal of our souls. It is not a payoff for being good, but a Vision we long to see. Heaven is a state and a place. It is the extraordinary gift of God. You and I will never, in this life, be able to comprehend what Heaven looks like or feels like, to know/ to imagine whether the music will be harpsichord or flute, or the awesome silence of God's loving gaze. Our mental pictures of the robes and the gardens and the clouds and the winged angels may be inadequate, but they're not foolish. They are merely the most we can do with the tiny glimpses of light we have received.

Heaven may seem difficult to understand, and that's okay. It's not easy to comprehend a place where everything is perfect, where sin cannot reign, where God is visibly present to us always. But we can never let the confines of our mind thwart our pursuit of the truth. Logic will give us a start on the matter, but only Faith, Hope, and Love can fill our minds with ideas and truths we could not otherwise grasp. If you pray to God for understanding, He will give it to you. If you say to Him, "Lord, help me to know what is true," you will come to know more than you ever imagined possible.

"Ask and you shall receive." You will be amazed at the light and insight God will give you, if only you will ask. You will realize that your confusion, your questions, and your skepticism all have a purpose: to bring you closer to God.

See you in Heaven!
(. . . I hope!)

Epilogue

THE PRAYER OF SAINT FRANCIS

Lord, make me an instrument of Your Peace.
Where there is hatred, let me sow love;
Where there is injury, pardon;
Where there is doubt, faith;
Where there is despair, hope;
Where there is darkness, light;
And where there is sadness, joy.

O Divine Master, grant that I may not so much
Seek to be consoled as to console,
To be understood as to understand,
To be loved as to love.
For it is in giving that we receive;
It is in pardoning that we are pardoned;
And it is in dying that we are born
To Eternal Life.

Amen.